Adventures in Archaeology

Tom McGowen
AR B.L.: 8.6
Points: 3.0   UG

SCIENTIFIC
AMERICAN *SOURCEBOOKS*

ADVENTURES IN ARCHAEOLOGY

TOM McGOWEN

 TWENTY-FIRST CENTURY BOOKS

A Division of Henry Holt and Company
New York

For Laura, Mike, Amanda, and Alex

Twenty-First Century Books / A Division of Henry Holt and Company, Inc. / *Publishers since 1866*
115 West 18th Street / New York, NY 10011

Henry Holt® and colophon are trademarks of Henry Holt and Company, Inc.

Henry Holt and Company, Inc., and Scientific American, Inc., are both wholly owned subsidiaries of Holtzbrinck Publishing Holdings Limited Partnership. Twenty-First Century Books, a division of Henry Holt and Company, Inc., is using the Scientific American name under a special license with that company.

The map featured in this book was created by Howard R. Roberts/HRoberts Design.

Library of Congress Cataloging-in-Publication Data
McGowen, Tom / Adventures in archaeology / Tom McGowen
p. cm.—(Scientific American sourcebooks)
Summary: Discusses some of the discoveries made by archaeologists around the world, including mummies found in Denmark and the sophisticated ancient city of Mohenjo-Daro in Pakistan.
1. Archaeology—History—Juvenile literature. 2. Antiquities—Juvenile literature. 3. Civilization, Ancient—Juvenile literature. 4. Excavations (Archaeology)—Juvenile literature.
[1. Archaeology. 2. Antiquities. 3. Civilization, Ancient.] I. Title. II. Series.
CC165.M26   1997   930.1—dc21   97-9755

ISBN 0-8050-4688-7
First Edition 1997

Printed in Mexico on acid-free paper ∞.
10 9 8 7 6 5 4 3 2 1

Photo Credits
pp. 6, 22, 30 (bottom), 35 (right): © Corbis-Bettmann; p. 8: Jonathan Blair/Woodfin Camp; pp. 9, 30 (top), 40: ©Scala/Art Resource, NY; p. 11: From John Frere "Account of Flint Weapons Discovered at Hoxne in Suffolk," *Archaeologia 13*/New York Public Library; p. 12: © DeSazo/Photo Researchers, Inc.; p. 14: © Heinz Plenge/Peter Arnold, Inc.; p. 15: © James L. Amos/Peter Arnold, Inc.; p. 17: © Aerofilms; p. 21: © UPI/Corbis-Bettmann; p. 21 (inset): © Rolf Adlercreutz/Gamma Liaison; p. 24: © D. Donne Bryant/Art Resource, NY; p. 27: From J. L. Stephens, *Incidents of Travel in Central America, Chipas, and Yucatán*, vol. 1, 1841/New York Public Library; p. 28: © Kenneth Garrett/Woodfin Camp; p. 34: © Kean/Archive Photos; p. 35 (left): © Robert Aberman/Barbara Heller/Art Resource, NY; pp. 37, 50, 63, 64, 76: © British Museum; p. 39: © Ashmoleon Museum, Oxford; p. 42: © Telegraph Colour Library/FPG; p. 44: © Dilip Mehta/Contact/Woodfin Camp; pp. 46, 60: © Erich Lessing/Art Resource, NY; p. 53: © David Matherly/Visuals Unlimited; p. 54: © Paul Hanny/Gamma Liaison; p. 56: © Forhistorisk Museum; p. 58: © Mark C. Burnett/Photo Researchers; p. 61: Photography by Egyptian Expedition, The Metropolitan Museum of Art; p. 66: © Wolfgang Kaehler/Gamma Liaison; p. 66 (inset): © Xinhua/Gamma Liaison; p. 68: © Patrick Landmann/Gamma Liaison; p. 70: Barry Iverson/Woodfin Camp; p. 73: © Bridgeman/Art Resource, NY; p. 78: From C. F. M. Textier, *Description de l'Asie Mineure*, 1839-49/Boston Public Library; p. 81: © Jeff Greenberg/Visuals Unlimited; p. 81 (inset): © Burrows/Gamma Liaison.

CONTENTS

INTRODUCTION

When most people think of archaeology, they seem to think mainly of tombs of Egyptian pharaohs, Egyptian mummies, Roman towns buried by volcanic eruptions, or ancient ruins in Greece. These are some of the best-known things associated with archaeology, so it may seem to most people as if all the important archaeological discoveries were made in either Egypt, Italy, or Greece.

But that isn't true. Exciting discoveries have been made in every part of the world—Africa, China, Central America, Europe, India, Japan, North America, South America, Pakistan. These discoveries simply aren't as well-known as the discoveries in Egypt, Greece, and Italy. While probably just about everyone is familiar with the mummies of Egypt, most people don't know of the 3,000-year-old natural mummies that have been found in Britain, Holland, Denmark, and Germany. Most people have heard of the marvelous treasures discovered in the tomb of the Egyptian Pharaoh Tutankhamen, but know nothing of the marvelously modern ancient city of Mohenjo-Daro, in Pakistan, where people had running water, baths, and toilets 4,500 years ago!

For that reason, this book covers archaeological discoveries and events all around the world, and not just in the places that are best known or where the most things were found. Thus, perhaps every reader of this book will learn of some important, exciting discovery that was made where his or her ancestors may have lived. For every one of us, no matter where our ancestors came from, has a heritage that goes back many thousands of years. Your ancestors may have created the awesome cave paintings of Europe; may have helped build the stone city of Great Zimbabwe, in Africa; may have fashioned the world's first pottery, in Japan; or may have helped construct the fabulous pyramids of Mexico. We can all be proud of the accomplishments of our ancestors of long ago, and it is archaeology that has given us almost everything we know about those people of ancient times.

Herculaneum

▼▼▼▼▼▼▼▼▼▼▼▼▼▼▼▼▼▼▼▼▼▼▼▼

ONE

DIGGING UP THE PAST

Archaeology is an old Greek word that basically means "ancient story." The science of archaeology attempts to learn the history of groups and nations of ancient people by means of the things they have left behind. Some of these things, such as the pyramids of Egypt and ruins of Rome, have been out in plain sight for thousands of years. But most things left by ancient people lie buried away beneath layers of earth, or in areas of wilderness, or in unknown caves, or under water. They have to be searched out, dug up, and studied. This is the basic work of men and women known as archaeologists.

In general, archaeologists look for three kinds of things, known as features, artifacts, and ecofacts. Features consist of such things as ruins of buildings, monuments, tombs, graves, and remains of ancient canals and roads: things that cannot be moved from the place where they are found. Artifacts are manufactured objects, such as tools, weapons, jewelry and art objects, coins, and clothing. Ecofacts are natural things such as bones or other remains of bodies, grain that was to be used as food, or the seeds of fruits that were eaten by people. Archaeologists also carefully study the location, known as the context, where any of these things are found, for this, too, can provide information about the way of life of the people who left these things behind.

The science of archaeology began in Europe during the time known as the Renaissance, or revival, from the 1300s to the 1600s, when education began to flourish and people became eager to discover more about their world. The ruins of the ancient buildings and structures of Greece and Rome, which had generally just been ignored for many hundreds of years, began to be investigated by scholars, historians, and people who simply felt they were beautiful. Here and there a statue or an art object was uncovered. Such things were known as antiquities, meaning, basically, "ancient objects." They were generally purchased by wealthy nobles, to become ornaments in gardens or rooms of palaces.

THE FIRST OF THE LOST CITIES   In the year 1709, a farmer in southwestern Italy began trying to dig a well on land that lay at the foot of the great volcano Mount Vesuvius. He uncovered a layer of marble blocks that seemed to be part of a buried building. Hearing of the farmer's discovery, a nobleman who lived nearby, Prince D'Elbeuf, bought the land and set workmen to digging in it. In addition to more marble blocks, they uncovered some beautiful statues and portions of carved stone pillars. No one yet knew it, but Prince D'Elbeuf's workers were opening up the remains of the ancient Roman town of Herculaneum, which had been buried under tons of ash and lava some 1,600 years earlier, during a terrible eruption of Mount Vesuvius.

Buried in the ash and lava that flowed from the eruption of Mount Vesuvius, Herculaneum was uncovered 16 centuries later.

Herculaneum was the first of many "lost cities" to be discovered. In 1748, digging began in an area a few miles away from Herculaneum, where some ancient statues had been found. Shortly, the ruins of a temple and other buildings were uncovered. In 1763, it was learned from some inscriptions found among the ruins, that these were the remains of the Roman city of Pompeii, which had also been buried by Vesuvius's ancient eruption. Meanwhile, in other parts of Italy, diggers were uncovering tombs of the ancient Etruscans, the people who controlled Italy about 2,400 years ago, before the rise of Rome. Out of these tombs came beautiful wall paintings, statues, and other works of art. All of these discoveries in Italy caused many Europeans and Americans to become interested in archaeology. Explorers—all men, in those days—began to set out for places where there were old ruins or ancient mounds that seemed as if they might contain buried antiquities.

This is a portion of a wall painting found in an Etruscan tomb. The figure on the left is making an offering; the other two are playing musical instruments.

THE DISCOVERY OF A TIME BEFORE HISTORY   At the time when the first discoveries of Herculaneum, Pompeii, and the Etruscan tombs were taking place, in the mid-1700s, most Europeans believed the world was only about 6,000 years old. This idea had been worked out by an Irish bishop, based on his calculations of dates for events mentioned in the Bible. It was also generally believed, even by historians, that people had always lived just about as they were doing in the 1700s, that is, that they had always lived in towns or cities, had always known how to make things out of metal, and had always depended mainly on farming for their food. But then, some events took place that made scholars and historians begin to realize that those beliefs were wrong.

The first event was the publication of an idea by a Scottish geologist (earth scientist) named James Hutton in 1788. Hutton described how the earth was constantly *changing*, with some areas of land being worn away by erosion—the action of wind, rain, floods, and flowing rivers—while other areas were being built up by earthquakes, volcanic action, and the formation of rock layers at the bottoms of seas. He pointed out that such changes took tens of thousands of years; therefore the earth had to be *much* older than just 6,000 years.

Then, in 1797, an English geologist, John Frere, discovered some sharp-edged cutting tools made from pieces of the kind of stone called flint, in a layer of gravel he was digging into. The tools had obviously been made by humans, but they were down in the ground well below a layer of sand containing the bones of some long-extinct animals. Geologists knew that the farther down in the earth a layer of rock was, the older it was, because all the layers above it had been slowly built up much later. So, Frere realized that the people who had made the stone tools had lived *before* the animals that had become extinct, which meant the people must have lived a very long time ago. Obviously, these people had not had metal or they wouldn't have had to make their tools out of stone. Frere could see that their way of life must have been very different from life as it then was in his time, the 1700s.

Eventually, Hutton's idea about the ever-changing earth, together with the discovery of very ancient, stone-using humans, changed people's minds about the age of the earth and the way people might have once lived. Scholars realized that there had been a "Stone Age" in prehistoric times (before any history was written), when people could not yet work metal and

The flint cutting tools found by John Frere in 1797 helped to establish the concept of a "Stone Age," when ancient humans led a life much different from that of people in the 1700s.

made their tools and weapons of stone, and probably got most of their food by hunting. In time, archaeologists decided there had actually been *three* prehistoric ages: a Stone Age; a Bronze Age, when people learned to melt copper and tin together to make the metal called bronze; and an Iron Age, when they began making things of iron.

DISCOVERING PREHISTORIC PEOPLE

Thus, people of the 1800s became aware that there had been humans living thousands of years before any of the historic events mentioned in the Bible. Interest grew when the first fossils of prehistoric people were actually discovered: the top of a skull and some leg bones, found in the Neander Valley of Germany in 1856, and some skeletons found in a French cave in 1868.

Then, in 1879, came the sensational discovery of magnificent paintings of animals made by prehistoric artists on the ceiling of a cave in Spain. At

Cave paintings found in Lascaux, France, and in other locations in Europe, changed archaeologists' ideas about what prehistoric people were like.

first, archaeologists thought the paintings were fake, done by a modern artist, for how could primitive, uncivilized Stone Age people create such beautiful art? However, in the 1890s, engravings and paintings were found in other caves, in France, and archaeologists began to realize that the people of prehistoric times were far more than just crude savages. The study of human prehistory became an important part of archaeology.

THE TREASURE SEEKERS   Meanwhile, mounds and ruins in the Near East and other parts of the world were being investigated. The men who first opened up many of these places were really just treasure seekers, looking for ancient art objects to sell to museums or wealthy collectors. When the treasure seekers began to excavate a ruin they would usually just pick a random point at which to start digging, and have their workers dig a trench straight in. One man even used huge charges of gunpowder to *blow* his way into one of the Egyptian pyramids! Obviously, these methods of excavation often damaged or destroyed parts of ruins and generally wiped out a lot of important information. For the ruins or remains of a place

▲ THE THREE AGES OF PREHISTORY ▲

The idea of the three ages—Stone, Bronze, and Iron—was developed in 1836 by a Danish museum curator named Christian Thomsen. It is very important to the study of human prehistory.

The Stone Age began about 2 million years ago when our primitive apelike ancestors learned how to chip stone, mainly flint, to make sharp-edged tools for cutting. Scientists divide the Stone Age into three parts: the Paleolithic (Old Stone Age), Mesolithic (Middle Stone Age), and Neolithic (New Stone Age). The Paleolithic era lasted from 2 million years ago to about 10,000 years ago, and during that time prehumans and humans learned how to make better and better tools of stone. By the time of the Mesolithic, people were making such things as flint daggers with wood and bone handles, beautiful smooth ax heads with holes in them for attaching to handles, and razor-sharp spearpoints shaped like laurel leaves.

At about the beginning of the Mesolithic Period, people in what is now Iraq began to make things of copper, a metal that could be picked up in nuggets along dry riverbeds. They found that it could be pounded into sharp-pointed tools as well as thin, flat sheets. And in time, they discovered that it could be melted and poured into molds to produce fine, sharp spearpoints and arrowheads, as well as disks and ornamental shapes for bracelets and necklaces. Then, about 5,500 years ago, people in the part of Iraq known as Sumer found that by melting copper with tin they could produce bronze, a much harder substance than copper. This was the beginning of the Bronze Age. With bronze, it was possible to make the first swords, as well as better armor and shields.

Finally, between 3,500 and 3,000 years ago in what is now Turkey, people discovered that when certain kinds of rocks were heated, a liquid flowed out of them that cooled into a dull black metal that was harder than bronze—iron. That was the beginning of the Iron Age. And actually, the Iron Age is the age in which most of us now live.

The three ages did not occur at the same time in every part of the world. While people in the Near East were making things of bronze, people in western Europe were still in the Stone Age, making most weapons and tools of stone. And there are even a very few people in the world today who are still living in a stone age.

where humans have lived for a long time nearly always have been built up in layers, with the oldest layer at the bottom, and each layer contains remains of the people who created it—things that they lost or threw away, such as tools or broken pottery. Carelessly digging into a top layer can badly disturb the layers below and jumble them together. As time passed however, the treasure seekers were replaced by men who realized the importance of digging carefully and trying to preserve everything they found for study, even bits of broken pottery. These men were the first true archaeologists.

ARCHAEOLOGY TODAY   When archaeologists of today begin to excavate, they use extreme care. They usually first make a map of the area (known as the site, or "dig"), take photographs, and write very precise descriptions of the surface of the site before any digging even begins. They may measure off small square sections of the site and dig neat square shafts, straight down. This is called stratigraphic digging, and serves to show exactly how far down the traces of human occupation go, and gives an idea of what each layer contains. The workers will generally take the soil of each layer they have dug up and sift it carefully through fine screens, in order to find such tiny things as beads, bits of broken pottery, seeds, and so on. These things can be very important in helping find out about the way of life of the people who once lived at the site.

This archaeologist is carefully recording the contents of a funeral chamber.

*T*he use of stratigraphic digging at archaeological sites helps to preserve important information about people of the past.

LOCATING BURIED TOMBS AND TOWNS

Most of the first places investigated by the treasure hunters and early archaeologists were clearly visible: big mounds, ruins of cities, or stone monuments. Today, there are ways of finding ancient things that may not be visible at all. Photographs of the ground taken from an aircraft directly overhead can reveal the presence of buried ruins, ancient roads and ditches, or burial mounds that have eroded away to almost nothing. Deep soil is usually thickly covered with vegetation, but soil that is shallow because there is something under it, such as an ancient stone wall, can support only a few plants, and shows up on an aerial photo as a streak that looks very different from everything around it. A slight swelling of a worn-down burial mound may not even be noticeable to a person standing right in front of it, but at sunrise and sunset it will cast a longish shadow that reveals it perfectly on a photo taken from above. The first aerial photographs that produced a major archaeological find were taken over the Sinai Desert in 1920. They showed that several ancient cities were lying beneath the sand! Today, in addition to standard aerial photography, archaeologists make use of special methods. Infrared photography can reveal buried objects. Photography from space can reveal details on the earth's surface that just aren't visible at closer distances. It can pick up the course of ancient roads and track them to the sites of buried cities.

There are also tools of modern technology that are helpful in searching for buried tombs and towns from the surface of the ground rather than the air. One of these is ground-penetrating radar, which sends radio waves into the ground. If the waves strike a buried object, they bounce back and form an image on a kind of television screen. Ground-penetrating radar is capable of such things as locating ancient communities that are buried under tons of volcanic ash. Another tool is a device known as a magnetometer. The earth has a magnetic field all around it, and a magnetometer can measure tiny differences in the field that are caused by such things as buried stone walls and buildings. A magnetometer can detect objects buried as deep as 15 feet (4.5 meters) underground.

Small objects can also be detected by means of modern technology. A military mine detector, designed to locate buried explosive devices, can be used to find such small metal objects as coins, arrowheads, and pieces of armor. In 1995, mine detectors were used to find the exact site of a 200-

Aerial photography can reveal the locations of previously undiscovered sites that have archaeological importance. Here it shows a royal Celtic monument in Ireland.

year-old American battlefield by locating buried weapons, uniform buttons, and bullets.

Computers, too, are an important tool used in archaeology today. They give modern archaeologists instant access to huge amounts of information that would have taken an "old-time" archaeologist months to sort through. Computers can do many special things, such as strengthening the image of faded writing painted on walls or weathered writing carved into stone, so that it can be read. They can even aid in the reconstruction of ruins by helping archaeologists make three-dimensional images of how the ruins may have looked.

ESTABLISHING THE AGE OF THINGS Naturally, archaeologists were always interested in trying to determine the *age* of things they found, from cities to skeletons. In the early days of archaeology, the age of some things could be figured out from historical records that go back about 6,000 years to the beginning of writing, but beyond that it was really impossible to establish an exact date for anything. Then, in 1949, there occurred what has been called the greatest breakthrough in the development of archaeology. An American scientist, Dr. Willard Libby, invented what is known as radio-carbon dating, which makes it possible to determine the age of once living things such as bones, wood, or leather. The bodies of all living creatures, plant or animal, contain a fixed amount of a chemical called carbon 14. When a plant or animal dies, the carbon 14 in its body begins to slowly

▲ **USING ARCHAEOLOGY TO** ▲
CORRECT WRITTEN HISTORY

Archaeology can sometimes be used to *correct* written history.

In 1794, a unit of the United States Army commanded by General "Mad Anthony" Wayne fought a battle against a force of Native Americans of the Miami Tribe in what is now the state of Ohio, near the city of Toledo. The soldiers won the battle, and peace was brought to the area, so that it was soon occupied by settlers from New York, Pennsylvania, and elsewhere, making new homes.

The place where the battle had been fought had no name. However, because of a great number of fallen trees lying about, General Wayne referred to the area in his report as "fallen timbers." Thus, the battle became officially known as the Battle of Fallen Timbers.

Eventually, after Ohio became a state in 1803, Ohioans wanted to commemorate the battle that had helped create their state. Stories handed down by the first settlers seemed to indicate that the battle had taken place at a point that is now between U.S. Highway 24 and the Maumee River, in an area of Toledo. A historical marker was placed there.

decrease at a steady rate per year. The radiocarbon dating process can measure the amount of carbon 14 left in bone, wood, leather, cloth, dried plant fiber, or other remains of once living things up to 70,000 years old. So when archaeologists now find the skeleton of a person in a prehistoric grave, they can determine when he or she died and thus tell how many thousands of years old the grave is.

The age of a tree can be told by counting the rings that show on a section of the trunk that has been cut. Thus, ancient objects made of wood can be dated by the rings on them. This is called dendrochronology. It can only be done with wooden objects less than 8,000 years old.

Things made of nonliving material, such as clay pots and statues, can also be dated. Scientists found that after a clay object was baked in a kiln, to make it hard, it would begin to store up energy from radiation given off by radioactive elements in the clay. This energy can be let loose in the form of light by burning a powdered piece of the pot, and the amount of light thus

But there were always doubts as to whether that place *was* the actual site of the battle. The stories of the old settlers did not agree on many points. And in recent years, historians began to believe that the battle might actually have been fought in another spot, which is now a farm field, about a mile away from where the marker was placed.

Historians know that battlefields are always covered with "litter" left over after a battle—remains of weapons, pieces of equipment, and other miscellaneous things. In 1995 a local college professor and a team of assistants began to examine the farm field with mine detectors. What they found were some 300 musket balls and many rifle bullets, of the kind fired by the muskets and rifles used in 1794; nearly forty metal buttons from soldiers' uniforms; and a bayonet, one of the long swordlike blades that fitted onto the end of a soldier's musket. This was definitely the litter of a battlefield! The methods of archaeology had shown that the farm field was indeed the place where the Battle of Fallen Timbers had actually been fought. History had been corrected. Local historians now intend to have the field given official recognition as the true battle site, and have it turned into a historical park.

released can be measured in a way that reveals how old the pot is. This process is known as thermoluminescence dating.

SUNKEN SHIPS AND SUBMERGED COMMUNITIES Remains of ancient civilizations and prehistoric life are found not only on land, but also underwater. As long ago as 1446, two sunken Roman ships were discovered at the bottom of Lake Nemi, in Italy, and an unsuccessful attempt was made to pull one of them up onto shore. Another attempt was made in 1827, but only fragments of wood and other bits and pieces were brought to the surface.

In 1853, a completely different kind of underwater find was made when the remains of a prehistoric village were detected in Lake Zurich, Switzerland. Archaeologists managed to pull up stone tools, bronze axes, bits of cloth, fragments of fishnets, and other objects. The village had stood on the shore of the lake almost 5,000 years earlier, but the lake had gradually covered it and had kept it covered. A drought in the 1850s shrank the lake, and parts of the village were revealed. Several other submerged villages were also found around this time.

As technology improved, underwater exploration and the "rescue" of sunken objects became easier. In 1900, divers recovered a number of statues from an ancient Greek ship lying on the seafloor near a Greek island. More statues, of bronze and stone, were brought up from other ancient sunken ships in waters off Greece in the 1920s. The remains of the Roman ships in Lake Nemi were finally raised in 1932, and they proved to be 1,900-year-old vessels of the time of the Emperor Caligula, which provided a wealth of information about Roman shipbuilding methods. In 1961, the Swedish warship *Vasa*, which sank in 1628, was raised to the surface and is now a museum of seventeenth-century life. And in 1984, the hull of a 3,400-year-old ship with a cargo of copper, tin, amber beads, woods, fruits, nuts, and spices was discovered in waters off the coast of Turkey. Sonar, a device that can detect underwater objects by bouncing sound waves off them, is used to locate such sunken ships. Underwater exploration is an important part of archaeology, adding vital information to our understanding of the past.

SEARCHING FOR REMAINS OF THE PAST Ever since the earliest days of archaeology, many discoveries have been made by sheer luck, by people who were not even archaeologists. Farmers digging wells have discovered buried cities and tombs. Children looking for a lost pet have found

The medieval warship Vasa was raised from Stockholm Harbor. The inset photo shows a portion of the magnificent ship after its restoration.

Roman mosaics were recently discovered in the center of Beirut, Lebanon. Reconstruction meant to repair damage caused by 15 years of civil war has uncovered amazing archaeological riches.

prehistoric cave paintings. Workmen digging foundations for new buildings or working beneath a city's streets have uncovered old graves, ruins of buildings of past communities, or relics of everyday life from previous times. When such lucky accidental finds are made, archaeologists are often notified and called on to use their skills and training to preserve the finds or to remove them so they may be studied. Thus, archaeology, unlike most sciences, can sometimes be a partnership between ordinary people and trained scientists.

But the majority of great archaeological discoveries have been made by trained professional archaeologists. Every year, in many parts of the world, teams of archaeologists set out to investigate places that they have good reason to believe will yield information about the past. If the site turns out to contain something of real importance, then the long, careful process of digging, sifting, cleaning, and studying begins. Most sites give up just a small amount of useful information about some era of the past, things that help fill out the knowledge of a particular place or people. But sometimes a major discovery is made—an unknown city, the tomb of a great leader of the past, or a hoard of ancient treasure. This is when the great adventure of archaeology reaches out to interest and excite everyone in the world with a sudden new burst of knowledge about the past that belongs to all of us!

*C*opán, Honduras

▼▼▼▼▼▼▼▼▼▼▼▼▼▼▼▼▼▼

TWO

LOST CITIES,
VANISHED EMPIRES

*T*he beginning of modern archaeology was a period of tremendous revelations and discoveries of places that had been lost from history—cities, kingdoms, and empires whose very existence had been forgotten or that had become no more than legends. Many of these places, especially in the Near East—the region made up of Egypt, Sudan, Turkey, the Arabian Peninsula, and Iran—had turned into great mounds covered by thousands of years of drifting sand, lying in parched desert areas. In Asia and Central America, many ruins of ancient cities were so covered over with jungle plants that they actually couldn't be seen. Often, these mounds and ruins were near present-day towns and villages, but the people of the modern communities paid no attention to them—they were simply part of the landscape.

The main discoveries of lost cities and vanished kingdoms began in the nineteenth century. At the beginning of the century, the only ancient cultures historians knew anything about were Greece, Rome, Egypt, and Persia. These had all left well-preserved ruins to study, and there was information about them in the Bible and in ancient Greek and Roman writings that could be read by scholars. The Bible also mentioned such ancient kingdoms of the Near East as Assyria and Babylon, but all traces of those seemed to have vanished completely. Nothing was known about the possibility of any ancient civilizations in Africa or Asia, and practically nothing was known about the civilizations that Spanish explorers had encountered in

Central and South America during the 1500s. But it was there that the first of the great nineteenth-century archaeological discoveries was made.

THE EMPIRE OF THE MAYANS   In the year 1836, a wealthy American lawyer named John Lloyd Stephens read of some strange ancient ruins that were said to be standing in the jungles of Central America. Stephens was intensely interested in collecting relics of ancient civilizations, and it seemed to him that these Central American ruins might well be a treasure trove of such things. He determined to go and investigate them.

It took several years to complete all the necessary preparations. But late in 1839, Stephens and a friend, a skilled English artist named Frederick Catherwood, were making their way through a steamy forest in the Central American country of Honduras. They were beginning to despair of finding anything in the seemingly endless green tangle. Then, one of their guides began to hack with his machete at a large vine-covered object in their path, and he revealed a tall pillar of stone covered with intricate carved designs and the figure of a man in fantastic clothing. The two explorers had never seen anything remotely like it.

Pushing on, Stephens, Catherwood, and their guides and workmen found many more such carved stone pillars. In ensuing days they began to encounter walls, stairways, and finally, pyramid-shaped buildings, all thickly overgrown with vines and plant life. The workers began to clear this away, and Catherwood set to work making drawings of everything. (Photography had not yet been perfected.) To make sure there was no trouble about what he was doing, Stephens actually *bought* the ruins, for fifty dollars, from a man in the nearby village of Copán, who owned the land on which the ruins stood.

What Stephens and Catherwood had found was a city of the ancient Mayan Empire, which had controlled a large area of Central America from about 1,800 to 1,100 years earlier. Actually, they had merely *re*discovered it, because Spanish explorers had originally found the ruins of this city and several others. However, news of those finds had simply been buried away. But when the two nineteenth-century explorers returned home, Stephens produced a book describing these ruins and others they later found and featuring the pictures Catherwood had made. In America and Europe, this news of a lost Central American civilization that had apparently been as great as Egypt or Assyria caused an explosion of interest. Archaeologists and explor-

Frederick Catherwood's detailed drawings recorded the Central American ruins discovered by John Lloyd Stevens. This drawing is of a column called a stela. Many such columns are found at the Copán site.

*T*he discovery of Copán, a city of the ancient Mayan empire, generated an explosion of interest in Mayan civilization.

ers began flocking to Mexico and Central and South America, and soon the marvelous story of Mayan civilization began to come to light.

THE FINDING OF THE ASSYRIANS The Old Testament of the Bible has a lot to say about the people known as Assyrians. They are described as a fierce, warlike folk who built a great empire, conquering the ancient kingdoms of the Israelites, Babylon, Syria, and even Egypt. But, in time, their empire was overcome and swept away. By the start of the nineteenth century, people knew only that the Assyrians had lived in Mesopotamia, which is now known as Iraq, but the whereabouts of their great cities mentioned in the Bible—Ninevah, Assur, Kalhu—were unknown. And nothing much was known beyond the biblical accounts about the Assyrian way of life, their art, their literature, or their appearance. Great Assyria and its inhabitants had simply vanished.

In 1843, Dr. Paul Emil Botta, a medical doctor, was a representative of the French government in Mesopotamia. Like John Lloyd Stephens, he was very much interested in ancient objects. The deserts of Mesopotamia were studded with many low hill-like mounds. Desert Arabs often dug ancient objects out of these mounds. One day, an Arab came to Dr. Botta and told him of a mound near a town called Khorsabad, that seemed to be filled with old things. Interested, Dr. Botta sent a few workmen to look at the mound and do a little digging. No more than a week later, a message came back to Botta, reporting that the mound was full of incredible finds!

Botta hurried there and found that the report was more than true. He did not know it yet, but his workers had unearthed nothing less than the palace of a king, Sargon II, which stood a short distance from one of the most important cities of the ancient Assyrian Empire, Ninevah. The digging went on for three years and brought forth household implements, weapons, slabs of stone carved with scenes of Assyrian life, and gigantic statues of bulls with heads of godlike bearded men and the wings of eagles. In 1845, a friend of Botta's, an Englishman named Austen Layard, began digging at the actual site of Ninevah. Among the things eventually uncovered was the great royal library, which contained letters, records of business transactions, historical documents, and works of literature. Thanks to the work of Botta and Layard, the story of Assyria, lost for some 2,500 years, was brought back to life.

*T*his winged statue, from the palace of Sargon II, was one of the artifacts uncovered by Dr. Paul Emil Botta at Khorsabad.

A reconstructed hall at Sargon's palace, restored under the direction of Austen Layard, is shown in this drawing. Note the winged statues on either side of the entryway.

TROY: THE LEGEND THAT BECAME FACT   One of the oldest stories that has come down to us from ancient times is the tale of the Trojan War. It tells of a time thousands of years ago, when an army of Greek warriors sailed across the Aegean Sea and besieged a great city known as Troy. The tale describes titanic battles as the Greeks tried to break into the city and the warriors of Troy defended it. Finally, the Greeks appeared to give up and sail away, leaving behind a huge statue of a horse carved of wood. Believing this to be a symbol of respect from the Greeks, the Trojan people hauled it into their city, rejoicing that peace had come.

But the horse was a trick. That night as the city slumbered, Greek soldiers hidden inside the horse emerged and opened the city gates to the Greek army, which had stealthily returned. The Greeks stormed into Troy and raged through the streets, slaughtering all the men, carrying the women and children off as slaves, and looting the city of all its treasures. Then they sailed away in reality, leaving the once great city a desolate, empty, burning ruin.

To most people of nineteenth-century Europe, this epic story was only a legend and the city of Troy was a place that had never really existed. But there were some people who felt that the legend of Troy was probably based upon an event that had really happened, and one of these was a wealthy German businessman named Heinrich Schliemann. When Schliemann was a child, his father had told him the story of the Trojan War, and the little boy had declared that he would someday find the place where Troy had been. He kept this goal all his life, and at the age of 41, a millionaire as a result of his business success, he retired and went to the coast of Turkey, across the Aegean Sea from Greece, to actually begin searching for the legendary city.

Schliemann soon became convinced that the site of Troy was near a Turkish town called Hissarlik that lay about an hour inland from the seacoast. There was a mound there, and Schliemann felt sure the ruins of Troy lay beneath it. He got permission from the Turkish government to excavate the mound, hired a hundred workers, and set them digging in April of 1870. Most archaeologists and historians who heard about what Schliemann was doing believed he was simply being foolish.

But the workers soon began to uncover ruins, and as they went deeper it became obvious that more than one city (actually, they were little more

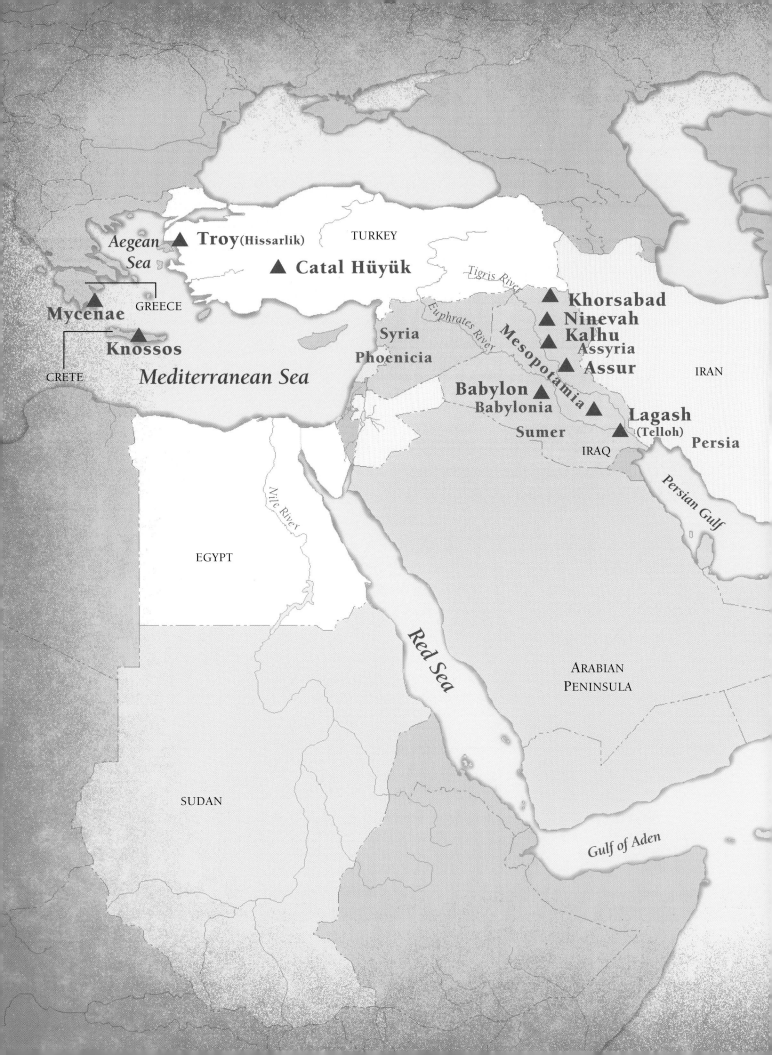

Aegean
Sea

▲ Troy (Hissarlik)

TURKEY

▲ Catal Hüyük

Tigris River

Euphrates River

▲ Khorsabad

▲ Ninevah

▲ Kalhu

Mesopotamia

Assyria

▲ Assur

Mycenae

GREECE

Syria

Phoenicia

▲ Knossos

CRETE

Mediterranean Sea

Babylon ▲

Babylonia

IRAN

Sumer

▲ Lagash
(Telloh)

IRAQ

Persia

Persian Gulf

Nile River

EGYPT

Red Sea

ARABIAN
PENINSULA

SUDAN

Gulf of Aden

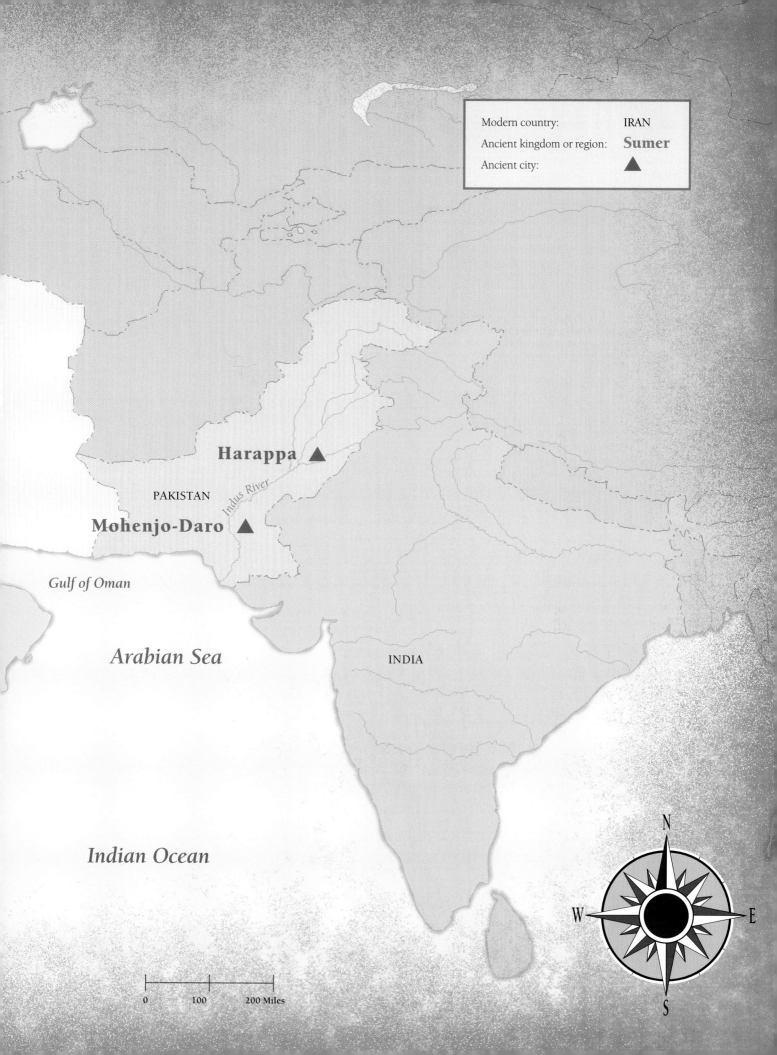

Modern country: IRAN

Ancient kingdom or region: **Sumer**

Ancient city: ▲

Harappa ▲

PAKISTAN

Indus River

Mohenjo-Daro ▲

Gulf of Oman

Arabian Sea

INDIA

Indian Ocean

0   100   200 Miles

N

W   E

S

*T*his engraving shows Greek soldiers emerging from the Trojan horse to open the city gates for their comrades.

than large villages) lay buried within the mound. At the end of three years the ruins of nine communities had been uncovered, one on top of another. And in one of these, beneath a section of stone wall, Schliemann himself found a pile of ancient treasure—bracelets, goblets, rings, earrings, and two crowns, all made of gold! The section of wall that covered the treasure was scorched black from fire. According to the story of Troy, the city had been burned by the Greeks, so Schliemann was convinced that *these* ruins were the remains of Troy and that he had found treasure hidden by someone when the city was attacked.

Archaeologists studied the ruins at Hissarlik, and today most scholars agree that one of the ruins *is* Troy, but they are not precisely sure which one. Regardless, Heinrich Schliemann had fulfilled his childhood vow and proven that Troy had been a real place and not a mere legend.

DISCOVERING THE BUILDERS OF GREAT ZIMBABWE   In the 1500s, Portuguese sailors did a great deal of exploring in Africa. Two of

these men wrote of finding a walled city, built entirely of stone, that stood somewhere deep in the southern part of Africa. Centuries later, in the 1800s, Europeans read these accounts and wondered. Did this city really exist? Could it be a lost city of some unknown ancient civilization? The Bible mentioned a land known as Ophir, a fabulous place of great culture and riches, that was somewhere in Africa. Could this stone city possibly be a city of Ophir? A few men began to search for it, hopeful of finding treasure.

In 1871, a German explorer by the name of Karl Mauch reached the area between the Limpopo and Zambesi Rivers in what is now the nation of Zimbabwe, looking for the ruined stone city. Eventually he found it, upon a high hill some miles from a small village. The walls and buildings, which included a 30-foot (9-meter) high cone-shaped tower, were built of large stone slabs fitted neatly together without mortar. Large carved soapstone birds adorned some of the buildings. The ruins were impressive. Mauch chose to believe that the city could not have been built by black African people. Instead he decided it must have been built by Phoenicians—a people similar to the Assyrians—who had erected stone cities in parts of the Near

Great Zimbabwe was an impressive walled city. Built of stone slabs fitted together without mortar, the city's fortifications included a cone-shaped tower.

East. He also became convinced that the stone city must have been the city of the woman mentioned in the Bible as the Queen of Sheba.

When Mauch returned to Europe and told of his find, his reports became widespread among people there, as well as throughout America. This was unfortunate, because a number of explorers, convinced they would find treasures of gold, began to flock to the region and dig among the ruins, causing serious damage. Eventually, in 1902, the government controlling the region had to pass a law to protect the ruins, which had become known as Great Zimbabwe. During the next forty years, only trained archaeologists were allowed to work in the city, looking for information rather than treasure. Items of the everyday life of the people who had lived in the city began to be found—pottery, tools, and weapons. And these turned out to be exactly like those that were produced by the African people who were living in this area. Thus, it was obvious that this great stone city had been built by native black Africans, and not by "Ophirians" or Phoenicians. Today, it is known that the builders of Great Zimbabwe were people known as the Shona, ancestors of people now living in the country of Zimbabwe, who began building the city around 900 years ago and created a vigorous empire that flourished for several hundred years.

THE DISCOVERY OF THE SUMERIANS

Not long after digging began on the ruins of the Assyrian city of Ninevah, some baked-clay tablets covered with a kind of wedge-shaped writing known as cuneiform were unearthed. They turned out to be a translation of words from an unknown language into the language of Assyria. In 1869, it was found that the unknown language was the tongue of a people who had lived in a region called Sumer. But these Sumerians were people about whom absolutely nothing was known. They had never even been heard of before.

In 1877, a French government official named Ernest de Sarzec examined a mound known as Telloh, in southern Mesopotamia (Iraq). He was excited to find that it was littered with inscribed bricks, fragments of pottery, and pieces of broken statues, and realized that it must be the remains of an ancient city. He had workmen begin excavating the mound, and in time they uncovered the ruins of buildings made of bricks of sun-dried mud, statues of people who looked nothing like Assyrians or Egyptians, and numerous clay tablets inscribed with writing in the language of the Sumerians.

Statues like this one were among the artifacts uncovered by Ernest de Sarzec. This represents the Governor of Lagash.

Sarzec was the first archaeologist to have discovered a city of ancient Sumer—the more than 4,500-year-old city of Lagash.

Sumer was not a kingdom but rather a group of independent cities inhabited by the same kind of people. Until 1869, no one had even suspected that Sumer ever existed, yet this was the oldest civilization of Mesopotamia. It was the place where cuneiform writing had been invented, where laws were first written down, and possibly even where the wheel had been invented. Most of the later civilizations of this part of the Near East—Babylon, Assyria, and the others—owed their way of life to ancient Sumer.

THE PALACE OF KING MINOS

An ancient Greek legend tells of a king named Minos who ruled the Greek island of Crete from a city called Knossos thousands of years ago. Minos possessed a monster known as the

▲ FROM BUSTLING CITY TO DESOLATE MOUND ▲

How could a thriving city of houses, temples, palaces, and thousands of people become nothing but a sandy mound or vine-covered ruin?

The deterioration would begin when the city was abandoned by its people. Sometimes, this was because of a terrible drought that dried up all the farmland around the city, forcing the people to abandon their homes and seek new lives somewhere else. Sometimes, it was the result of war. When an enemy army captured a city, most of the city's men were slaughtered, while the women and children would be rounded up and marched off to become slaves, leaving the city empty.

Most ancient cities of the Near East were built of bricks formed of dried clay, which continued to dry out in the intense heat of the sun and gradually crumbled away. While the city was inhabited, crumbling bricks were simply replaced, or often a crumbling house was just demolished and a new one built on top of the old foundation (which caused the city to actually grow higher over hundreds of years, with the lower parts of it formed of layers of old brick). But once the city was abandoned, bricks crumbled away into fragments and powder, and buildings slowly collapsed, with the upper parts falling in and burying the lower parts under piles of rubble. Over the centuries, a great mound slowly formed as desert winds dropped tons of sand.

In hot, wet parts of the world such as Thailand and Central America, where jungles flourish, it was also easy for abandoned cities to get "lost." Most of the ancient cities in these places were built of rock, and jungle plants swiftly took root among the abandoned rocks and soon covered them with a leafy, tangled growth that hid the cities from sight.

Minotaur, half man and half bull, kept in a huge building that was a maze, with so many branching tunnels that no one could find a way out once inside. Each year, seven young men and seven young women were forced into the maze to become sacrifices to the Minotaur. One year, however, the Greek hero Theseus entered the maze and, meeting the Minotaur in a darkened tunnel, killed it. He then escaped from the maze by following a trail of thread he had unrolled when he entered.

In 1893, Sir Arthur Evans, head of the Ashmolean Museum of Oxford University, in England, found some tiny stone seals in a little curiosity shop in Greece. They were obviously very old and appeared to be inscribed with what looked like some kind of writing. The seals had come from Crete, and to Evans they seemed to be a hint that something of importance might be hidden away there. In 1894, he visited the island and investigated the mound of Knossos, on the northern coast. In 1900, he led an expedition to Crete and began to dig at Knossos. Shortly, he saw that his workers were uncovering the ruins of a great palace.

Evans thought the palace was a relic of what was known as the Mycenaean civilization of Greece, which dates back to around 3,500 years ago. But as the digging continued, it revealed that the origin of this palace went back a good deal farther than that. Evans realized that he had discovered a civilization that, like Sumer, historians had not known of.

Sir Arthur Evans discovered an enormous palace at Knossos in northern Crete.

*T*he Palace of Knossos was evidence of a previously undiscovered civilization—a civilization
Arthur Evans named "Minoan."

It needed a name. The many rooms and corridors of the palace were
almost like a maze, and that made Evans think of the legend of King Minos
and the Minotaur. And so, he began to refer to this newly discovered civilization as "Minoan," after King Minos.

The palace was virtually a small city that sprawled over an area of more
than 700,000 square feet (210,000 square meters) and was occupied by
probably as many as 5,000 people. It had been a major trading center of the

Aegean Sea. Beneath the palace, Evans found storerooms, still containing huge, beautifully decorated jars that had held olive oil. The walls and ceilings of the palace rooms had been brightly painted with scenes and decorations, and much of the painting was still bright and fresh-looking. One of the most famous wall paintings found at Knossos shows a young man and woman performing some kind of acrobatics with a huge bull. Could this have something to do with the Minotaur legend?

Sir Arthur Evans continued to oversee the digging at Knossos for a number of years, and used much of his own money to help restore the ruins. Like Heinrich Schliemann, he had shown that a legend could contain a core of fact.

MYSTERY CITY OF THE INCAS

Discoveries of lost cities continued into the twentieth century. In 1911, Hiram Bingham, an American, led an expedition into the Andes Mountains of Peru, searching for a legendary city of the Inca Empire, known as Vilcabamba. The Incas were a South American Indian people who created an empire that extended along the western coast of South America, including parts of present-day Argentina, Bolivia, Chile, Colombia, Ecuador, and Peru. The Spanish explorer Francisco Pizzaro conquered and destroyed this empire in 1532. Vilcabamba had been one of the last Inca cities to fall.

Bingham and his party made their way deep into the wild, thickly forested Urubamba Valley, up in the Andes, with mountain slopes rising on all sides. They stayed for a while in a village of the Quechua people, and one of the men told Bingham that there were ruins nearby. When Bingham asked where they were, the man pointed straight up, at the rising slope of the mountain known as Machu Picchu.

For half a dollar—actually, a fairly sizable amount of money in those days—Bingham hired the man to take him up to the ruins. On July 24, 1911, Bingham, the Indian guide, and the bodyguard given to Bingham by the Peruvian government, Sergeant Carrasco of the Peruvian Army, began the ascent. First, they crossed the rushing torrent of the Urubamba River on a rickety bridge made of a few logs tied together. Then they climbed the sloping mountainside, grasping vines and tree branches to haul themselves up the narrow, almost invisible trail.

Two thousand feet (600 meters) up, they reached the top and came

*T*he purpose of Machu Picchu is unknown, but these *amazing ruins perched high in the Andes mountains are clear evidence of the skills of the site's original builders.*

upon the hut of a Quechua family that had a small farm there. The family's little boy, about 10 years of age, led Bingham and his bodyguard through a patch of trees, and the American suddenly found himself looking at an amazing array of stone ruins overgrown by vegetation, spread out upon the mountain ridge. He saw a great stairway, dozens of houses, an imposing tower, and the remains of what must have been temples. They were formed of blocks of granite, perfectly fitted together without mortar.

Hiram Bingham thought he had found Vilcabamba, but he had not; that was discovered 53 years later. These ruins became known as Machu Picchu, but the original name of the community is unknown. Machu Picchu is somewhat of a mystery, for there is no record of its origin or purpose. It is actually too small to have been a city, and scholars now think it may have been a religious community, perhaps somewhat like a medieval European monastery. But it is an awesome monument to the building skills of the Inca architects and workers who constructed it.

MOHENJO-DARO, THE LOST CITY OF PAKISTAN   In 1921 and 1922, excavations were begun at mounds known as Harappa and Mohenjo-Daro, on the Indus River in Pakistan, which was then part of India. Cities were uncovered at both places, but the one at Mohenjo-Daro was by far the better-preserved of the two. It was a very large, 4,500-year-old city that had been carefully laid out with straight, narrow streets paved with baked clay bricks and lined with windowless brick houses. These houses had bathrooms with a water supply and drain, for bathing, and even primitive toilets. The city had a granary (grain storage building), a large public bathhouse, and two large buildings that archaeologists named "the College" and "the Assembly Hall." It was fortified against attack, with walls and watchtowers. Unearthed from the city's ruins were bronze and baked-clay figurines of men and women, pottery, and a great many carved stone seals and clay tablets containing symbols that were obviously a form of writing.

Since Harappa and Mohenjo-Daro were discovered, a number of much smaller but similar cities have been found in this region of Pakistan and across the border in India. Clearly, a great ancient civilization flourished there between 4,500 and 3,500 years ago. Unfortunately, the writing on the clay tablets has not been deciphered and probably never can be, so we may never know what these people called themselves, nor much more about them than what the ruined cities revealed.

*A*rchaeologists continue to search the ruins at Mohenjo-Daro for new artifacts—and new information.

An 8,300-Year-Old City in Turkey

In 1961, at a mound called Catal Hüyük in central Turkey, British archaeologist James Mellaart uncovered the oldest unknown city yet found. Perhaps as much as 8,300 years old, it was a city of flat-roofed mud-brick buildings packed tightly against one another. There were small courtyards among the buildings, but there were no streets, and the sides of the outermost buildings formed a single solid wall, enclosing the entire city. The entrances to the houses were on the roofs, reached by ladders. The interior walls of many of the buildings were colorfully decorated. The several thousand people who once lived there had tools of stone and bone, baskets and mats of woven plant stems, bowls and boxes of carved wood, and cloth. They did not have any form of writing.

Other lost cities and forgotten cultures were found in other parts of the world in the twentieth century, including the Inca city of Vilcabamba, in Peru, and the kingdom of Dvaravati, in Thailand. And it is quite likely that still other cities and the remains of other unknown civilizations are even now lying hidden somewhere, silently waiting to be found.

The inlaid gold mask of Tutankhamen

▼▼▼▼▼▼▼▼▼▼▼▼▼▼▼▼▼▼▼▼▼▼▼▼▼▼▼

THREE

TOMBS, GRAVES, BONES, AND BODIES

*I*n the year 1922, an Englishman named Howard Carter crouched in darkness among stone ruins beneath the desert in Egypt. He had knocked a hole in a door and pushed a candle through the hole to peer into a room that had been hidden in darkness for more than 3,200 years. "Can you see anything?" a man behind him questioned eagerly. Carter answered in a voice that shook. "Yes, wonderful things!" He was peering into the tomb of an ancient king, and it was filled with objects that glittered and glowed in the candlelight. He could make out statues, furniture, chests, vases, jewelry—a wealth of things that had been fashioned by artists and craftsman 32 centuries earlier. A treasure trove of information about ancient Egypt had been discovered!

Many of the greatest finds of archaeology, things that have provided vast information about the ways of life of people who lived thousands of years ago, have come from places where people buried their dead. For it is generally a custom of humans to bury the dead dressed in their finest clothing and accompanied by at least some of the things that the dead person used or cherished in life. Thus, the tombs of great rulers of ancient times are often filled with treasures that had belonged to the ruler, and graves of ordinary people may contain items of clothing and personal belongings—jewelry, weapons, and drinking cups. Archaeologists call such things "grave goods." From graves, tombs, bones, and bodies has come much of our knowledge of the past.

STONE AGE GRAVES   Most of our primitive human ancestors did not bury their dead. They simply left them lying where they died. Generally, the bodies were eaten by animals, and parts of them were often carried off, so it is almost impossible to ever find a complete skeleton of one of these prehistoric people. The bones that have been found can tell us much about the physical appearance and abilities of the people, but they can tell us almost nothing about how the people lived. Complete skeletons of people buried in graves, however, can often tell us a great deal.

The custom of burying the dead seems to have begun with the kind of humans known as Neanderthals, who lived from about 100,000 to 35,000 years ago in the time known as the Paleolithic, or Old Stone Age. The first of their graves to be discovered, in France in 1908, contained the skeleton of a teenage boy who had died about 50,000 years earlier. He had been put into the grave lying on his side, with his legs drawn up and a hand under his cheek, as if asleep. Apparently a cutting tool of chipped flint had been put into the grave with him. A number of similar graves have been found, and the skeletons of some of the people show signs that they were badly crippled during their lifetimes. These people could not have survived unless someone had taken care of them. All this seems to show that the Neanderthals, who were physically different from us in several ways, must have had a feeling of care for each other and for their dead that earlier kinds of humans did not have.

Humans of our species—people who were exactly like us—appeared on the earth about 35,000 years ago, near the end of the Old Stone Age. They, too, buried their dead, and generally put them into their graves fully clothed and with some of their personal belongings. Thus, the many graves that have been found from that time have greatly helped archaeologists form a picture of what life was like at the end of the Old Stone Age.

A 23,000-year-old skeleton of a man found in a grave in Russia was covered with hundreds of beads made of carved ivory from mammoth tusks. The beads had undoubtedly been attached to animal-skin (leather) clothing of some sort that had rotted away. He had also been wearing a beaded headband and apparently a necklace and armlets of animal teeth. A 20,000-year-old grave in Italy held the skeletons of two young children who had obviously been buried in clothing to which hundreds of small seashells were attached. From finds such as these, archaeologists can tell that some of these prehistoric people—whom we generally think of as half-naked "cave men" with shaggy animal skins wrapped clumsily around their waists—actually wore clothing that was painstakingly and probably artistically decorated, as well as many kinds of jewelry. It is also apparent that the people who had such things—and not all did—must have been wealthy by the standards of their time, and this could indicate that they were people of importance, such as chieftains and the wives and children of chieftains. Thus, many archaeologists believe that the people near the end of the Old Stone Age had created what is known as a ranked society—a society ruled by noble families, like the families of kings, dukes, and other nobles in historical times.

Graves such as these also give evidence that people of the late Stone Age were buried with rituals—what we might call funeral services. A large amount of red powder made of ground iron ore had been poured over the body of the man in the Russian grave, and traces of the same kind of red powder have been found in many other late Stone Age graves all over Europe. The exact meaning of this is unknown, of course—although some archaeologists think the redness may have represented blood—but it does seem to show that even as long as 25,000 years ago humans were giving their dead some kind of last rites before sealing their graves. This indicates that religion played a part in people's lives even then.

Burials of the bodies of Stone Age people have given archaeologists a great deal of information. But there was another way ancient people disposed of their dead. Called mummification, it provides facts mere skeletons could never reveal.

THE MUMMIES OF ANCIENT EGYPT   Between 12,000 and 7,000 years ago, the Stone Age people of Egypt were burying their dead in shallow pits in the desert, usually with a few clay pots, some beads, and items of food and drink. The hot, dry sand quickly soaked all moisture out of the bodies, and they were preserved, with the skin, now as tough as leather, shrunk over the bones. This is probably what gave Egyptians the idea of deliberately mummifying bodies, for they had come to believe that a dead person's body had to be preserved in order for the person to be able to live an immortal life-after-death in the world of the gods. Thus, mummifying dead bodies was a basic part of Egyptian religion.

Deliberate mummification of the dead began in Egypt about 5,000 years ago and continued for several thousand years. During that time, Egyptian embalmers, the men who mummified dead bodies, naturally

This mummy, known as "Ginger," dried naturally in Egypt's hot, dry sand. Note the presence of simple grave goods buried with the body.

learned a great deal about preserving the dead, and methods of mummification changed over the centuries. But basically, the body was embalmed and then tightly wrapped in many layers of cloth. For a long time, only the bodies of kings and queens were mummified, and put into elaborate tombs with large amounts of costly and beautiful items for use in the afterlife. Gradually, nobles and high-ranked officials were mummified after death as well, and finally, after many centuries, common people were also allowed to be mummified. However, the poorer commoners' bodies were usually just wrapped in linen sheets and put into shallow pits in the desert with a few of their belongings.

Although almost all the tombs of Egyptian kings and nobles were robbed of most of the things in them many thousands of years ago, the mummies themselves have often been a source of information about ancient Egyptian arts and crafts. From mummies that have been unwrapped have come such things as perfectly preserved sandals, painted face masks,

▲ ADVENTURES OF AN EARLY ARCHAEOLOGIST ▲

One of the first archaeologists, who secured many prized relics of ancient Egypt for the British Museum, in London, began his career as a circus strong man!

Giovanni Belzoni was born in Padua, Italy, in 1778. He grew up to be nearly 6 feet, 7 inches (1.97 meters) tall and extremely strong. So, as a young man he became a strong man, entertaining people with feats of strength at fairs and circuses. In 1803, Belzoni took his act to England and became very popular for a time.

But eventually his popularity faded and he had to find another way of making a living. He went to Egypt in 1815 to try to sell the Turkish governor of Egypt an irrigation device he had invented. The governor was not interested, but Belzoni became acquainted with the British Consul of Egypt, Henry Salt, who was eager to secure relics of ancient Egypt for the British Museum. Belzoni was given the job of traveling up the Nile River to look over a huge stone head of an ancient pharaoh and judge if he could manage to transport it back down the river for shipment to England. He was able to do so, in spite of some tremendous difficulties.

Belzoni spent the next four years scouring Egypt for relics for the museum. He made some major discoveries. It was he who found the awesome tomb of Pharaoh Seti I, in the region known as the Valley of Kings. He also discovered the hidden chamber in the great Pyramid of Chephren—and wrote his name on one of the walls.

Giovanni Belzoni was a very poorly educated man with absolutely no scientific training, and some of his ways of doing things caused damage and destruction. But he was sincerely interested in trying to collect useful information rather than simply treasure hunting. He kept good records of the things he saw in the places he investigated—paintings, sculptures, pottery, even the way mummies had been placed. A surprisingly skillful artist, he made some fine sketches of tomb paintings, stone carvings, and other things that were later of help to scholars. When Belzoni returned to England in 1819, he was widely acclaimed for his work. Most of the relics he brought back now form a large display in the British Museum.

bracelets, and other forms of jewelry. And from the preserved bodies of mummies has come considerable information about the quality of life in ancient Egypt. Medical experts examining Egyptian mummies have found that the ancient Egyptians must have been generally rather sickly because of many kinds of parasites, such as various kinds of worms, that infested their bodies and caused sores, rashes, weakness—and shortened lives. The Egyptians also had lung problems, caused by constantly breathing sand blown in from the desert. They had arterial disease, too, similar to that suffered by many people today. However, they do not seem to have been affected by most kinds of cancer.

As new medical and biological technologies become available, archaeologists are continuing to learn new facts about ancient Egypt from the mummified bodies of its people. Just recently, checks of DNA found in mummified bodies in a certain region of Egypt have revealed that many of the dead belonged to the same families, going back a number of generations.

THE MUMMIES OF SOUTH AMERICA   Like the Egyptians, the Inca people of South America buried their dead in hot, dry desert areas, as well as in cold, dry caves high in the mountains. In both places, bodies became naturally mummified, and thus the Incas learned about mummification. Some 5,000 years ago, they began deliberately mummifying their dead. But unlike the Egyptians, the Incas did not begin by preserving only their kings, they mummified everyone, because they believed that everyone could have an immortal life-after-death if they were mummified.

In general, a dead person was put into a seated position in a large, shallow basket, with knees drawn up to the chest and hands placed flat upon the face. Dressed in its best clothing and jewelry, the seated body was covered with layers of cloth tied in place with woven cloth cords, forming a big, bulky bundle. Because there are so many such mummies to be found, archaeologists have been able to learn a great deal about the Incan Empire. Clothing with beautifully woven patterns and gold jewelry and ornaments with intricate designs have come out of Inca mummy wrappings. Beautiful pottery, weapons, and preserved remains of foods such as corn, beans, and potatoes, have been found in tombs where mummies had been placed.

Medical examinations of Incan mummies have shown that the Incas of several thousand years ago, like the ancient Egyptians, suffered from parasites in their bodies. Some of them had the same kinds of worms that trou-

PROCEDENCIA   PARACAS
SEXO   MASCULINO
EDAD   25 - 30 AÑOS

The Incan people of South America mummified all their dead, both royalty and commoners.

bled the Egyptians. The examinations also revealed that Incan doctors apparently tried to cure certain diseases by means of operations on the head—cutting out a piece of a person's skull. Modern doctors can tell that many Incas seem to have survived such operations, and some had even been operated on more than once. Examinations made of mummies from before and after the Spanish explorers destroyed the Incan Empire showed that those who lived after the Spanish takeover did not eat as well, and were not as healthy as those who lived before the Spaniards' coming.

THE MUMMIES OF EUROPE: THE "ICEMAN" AND THE BOG PEOPLE

One of the greatest archaeological finds of the twentieth century was the result of the natural mummification of a human by freezing. In 1991, the preserved body of a man who had died 5,100 years ago, during the New Stone Age, emerged from a melting glacier in a region of Italy in the Alps Mountains. The man had apparently suffered an injury—several of his ribs were broken—and was in poor physical condition. He was probably caught out in the open by the sudden onset of winter weather in the moun-

The body of the "Iceman" remained frozen and mummified within a glacier for more than 5,000 years.

tains, perhaps a blizzard, and must have crawled into a crevice to seek shelter. There, he died of exposure. Covered by a thick blanket of snow, his body had quickly frozen. Eventually encased in tons of ice, it remained frozen and mummified for 5,100 years.

Not only was the man's body preserved by the ice, but so were his clothing and possessions, providing a treasure trove of information about Stone Age life. He had been dressed in a kind of tunic, leggings, and shoes of animal skin, a cone-shaped fur cap, and a thick cloak made of plaited (braided) dried grass. He had carried a copper ax with a wooden shaft, and a bow and leather quiver of arrows. In a fur pouch slung from his belt of twisted leather, he had kept tools made of stone and bone, for cutting, slicing, punching holes, and sewing; a net made of woven grass, probably for catching birds; and a chunk of flint and piece of iron ore, for making sparks to start a fire. He had even possessed medicine: two dried mushrooms of a kind now known to contain a high amount of a substance that can help prevent certain infections. Apparently, its medical value was known in his time, too.

Finding the body and possessions of this man of 5,100 years ago as it emerged from the ice and before everything decomposed was an incredible piece of luck. It has given us knowledge of Stone Age clothing, craftsmanship, technology, and lifestyle that could not have been gained in any other way.

▲　　▲　　▲

In addition to being preserved by extreme dryness and freezing, human bodies can also be naturally mummified in the ooze of a bog. A bog is an area of wet, spongy earth containing a large amount of partly decayed vegetation that is called peat. There are chemicals in bog water that prevent plant and animal remains from decaying as quickly as usual. Nearly seven hundred preserved bodies, mostly of ancient people, have been recovered from bogs in the British Isles, Denmark, Holland, and Germany over the past 150 years. These bodies have become known as the "bog people."

Most of the bodies that have been studied seem to be between 2,000 and 3,000 years old, from the beginning of the Iron Age. They have most, if not all, of their skin, although it is, of course, badly shrunken over the bones. Generally, their fingernails and toenails still exist. Most have hair, and on several the hair was tied or braided as it was in life. One man, found at Lindow Moss bog, in England, had a beard and mustache. In some cases, such as the Lindow Man and the Tollund Man of Denmark, the shrunken stomach and intestine remained, with bits of food preserved in them. Well-preserved articles of clothing, made of wool and animal skin, were recovered with some of the bodies.

A disturbing thing about most of these ancient people is that they appear to have died violent deaths. Many had apparently been strangled or hanged, and the ropes were still around their necks. Nearly all had head wounds made by clubs or axes. The Danish Borremose Man had been both axed and strangled, the Danish Graubelle Man had been strangled and had his throat cut, and the Lindow Man had been axed, strangled, *and* had his throat cut!

This bog body, known as Tollund Man, shows an amazing degree of preservation. A noose was found around the mummy's neck.

A few of these people had probably been murdered, perhaps by robbers, and their bodies were thrown into a bog to hide the crime. But it looks as if a number of them were executed for crimes they might have committed. And it seems clear that some of them, such as the Lindow Man, Tollund Man, and Graubelle Man, were human sacrifices! It is apparent that the bogs these people were taken from were considered holy places, for a great many things have been found in them that obviously were put there as offerings—pots of food, weapons, and items made of gold and silver. From Roman writings it is known that the ancient Celtic and Germanic peoples who lived near these bogs practiced human sacrifice as part of their religions. And there are indications that many of the bog people may well have been specially selected persons who may have willingly given up their lives as part of a religious ritual. They appear to have been nobles, for they have fine features, and their hands have no calluses as do the hands of hardworking commoners. Also, examinations of their stomachs showed that some of them had eaten what may have been a special "last meal" of herbs and cereals as part of a ritual.

STONE AGE CEMETERIES AND TOMBS About 6,200 years ago, the people of Europe began creating cemeteries—areas of land where, apparently, all the members of a community were buried generation after generation. A number of these sites have been found by archaeologists. One of the most noticeable things about them is that many of the people buried in them were obviously killed by pointed weapons such as spears and arrows. Many of the skeletons still have missile points embedded in their bones. It looks very much as if these people might have been fighting wars.

Between 6,000 and 3,500 years ago, people of western Europe and several other parts of the world constructed numerous tombs that were marked by large mounds of earth. Some of these were simply the grave of a single person, buried in a shallow pit or laid on the ground, then covered with a round mound of piled-up earth. Others were long hallways in which 200 or more bodies might be buried, formed of rows of very large stones covered with a long, high earth mound. Still others were long hallways that led into large stone-walled rooms where bodies were piled atop one another. From all these types of mound-tombs have come such things as decorated baked-clay drinking cups and cooking pots, beautifully made razor-sharp flint daggers, ax heads of polished stone, and many kinds of jewelry. The tombs and grave goods have helped archaeologists form a clear picture of what life was like in Europe in the last centuries of the Stone Age.

THE MOUND BUILDERS OF NORTH AMERICA

North America also has grave mounds. They were built over a period of some 7,000 years by several Native American cultures, and some of them are more spectacular than the prehistoric monuments of both Europe and the Near East. A mound known as Monk's Mound, at Cahokia, Illinois, rises 100 feet (30 meters) in height and has a base wider than that of any of the Egyptian pyramids. The Great Serpent Effigy Mound of Ohio has the long, sinuous, curving shape of a snake; 5 feet (1.5 meters) high, 20 feet (6 meters) thick, and 1,330 feet (399 meters) long. In Wisconsin, there is a turtle mound, a flying swan mound, lizard mounds, and a mound in the shape of a man, 210 feet (63 meters) long. Like the Old World mounds, many American mounds have been found to contain skeletons and grave goods, such as carved stone pipes, tools made of hammered copper, and jewelry made of silver, volcanic glass, and mica, a mineral that can be split into thin shiny sheets.

Seen from above, the Great Serpent Effigy Mound stretches for nearly a quarter of a mile.

In 1780, before he was U.S. president, Thomas Jefferson made what was actually the world's first modern-type archaeological dig, into a small mound near his home in Virginia. He examined some of the bones in the mound and wrote a full description of how the mound was constructed. In later years, a few others began to investigate mounds. Unfortunately, during the nineteenth century, many mounds were simply plundered by treasure seekers and collectors. Much crucial information was destroyed as a result.

THE ROYAL TOMBS OF MYCENAE   The ruins of the 3,300-year-old city of Mycenae, in Greece, were quite visible in 1876, when Heinrich Schliemann, the discoverer of Troy, began to excavate them. According to the ancient story of the Trojan War, a king of Mycenae, Agamemnon, was leader of the Greek warriors that fought against Troy. When Agamemnon returned home after Troy's destruction, he and his companions were murdered by traitors and their bodies thrown into a common grave. This event, like the story of the Trojan War, was considered a legend by most people. But what Schliemann was digging for at Mycenae was nothing less than the grave of Agamemnon.

Schliemann began excavating in August of 1876. He believed that the ancient story indicated exactly where the graves must be, and that was where he had his men dig. Unfortunately, in his burning desire to find the graves, he took shortcuts and used methods that resulted in destruction and damage to some of the ruins. But on December 6, the diggers uncovered a grave that had been dug deep into the rock upon which Mycenae stood. And in ensuing weeks they found four more. Within these graves were fifteen skeletons and a treasury of gold and silver objects and weapons. Several of the skeletons were wearing golden masks that might have been portraits of what the men's faces had looked like when they were alive.

Schliemann was convinced he had indeed found the graves of Agamemnon and his murdered companions. But it is now known that the bodies he found were buried some 300 years before the time when the Trojan War is supposed to have taken place. However, Schliemann's discovery caused other archaeologists to begin working at Mycenae and other ruins of Bronze Age Greece, uncovering important information. The treasure he discovered in the Mycenaean graves was the richest treasure yet uncovered by an archaeologist, and showed that the legends of Mycenae as a city of vast wealth may well be true.

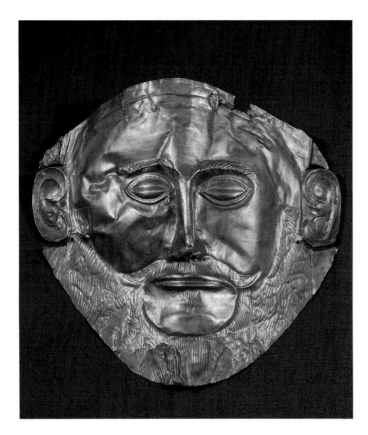

This golden mask was found in what Heinrich Schliemann believed was the tomb of Agamemnon.

THE TREASURES OF TUTANKHAMEN

Many of ancient Egypt's greatest and most powerful pharaohs (kings) were buried in hidden, underground tombs in a rocky desert region known as the Valley of Kings. It was the Egyptian custom to fill a pharaoh's tomb with things to make his afterlife as pleasant as his earth life had been, so these dead kings were buried with enormous amounts of furnishings and treasures. When nineteenth-century scholars became able to read Egyptian hieroglyphics, they learned the names of all these kings, and archaeologists soon began searching for the tombs. By 1920, all the tombs but one had been located. However, in every case, most of the things that had been buried with the king were gone. The tombs had been located by tomb robbers thousands of years ago, and all treasure had been carried away.

The one tomb that had not been found was that of a pharaoh named Tutankhamen, who had ruled Egypt some 3,200 years ago. He had not been a very important monarch, however, and most archaeologists thought his tomb might be small and impossible to find. But British archaeologist Howard Carter believed he knew exactly where to look. Some objects clearly marked with Tutankhamen's name had been found near the tomb of the Pharaoh Ramses VI. This was where Carter had his workmen start digging.

They dug in various spots for six years and found nothing. Finally, the man paying for all this work, Lord Carnarvon of England, told Carter to give up. But Carter persuaded Carnarvon to let him make one last try. In early November of 1922, he had his men dig into the ruins of some huts of ancient tomb workers that were at the very foot of the Ramses VI tomb. To his elation, a rubble-filled stairway was revealed.

Carter and his workmen cleared a way down the stairs. At the bottom was a walled-up door. Now Carter had to wait more than two weeks while Lord Carnarvon came from England. Then, the workmen broke through the door and spent several days digging through a stone-filled tunnel, at the end of which was another sealed door. On the other side of this was the room that Carter saw when he put the lighted candle into the hole and peered in—a room filled with things put there for Tutankhamen's afterlife.

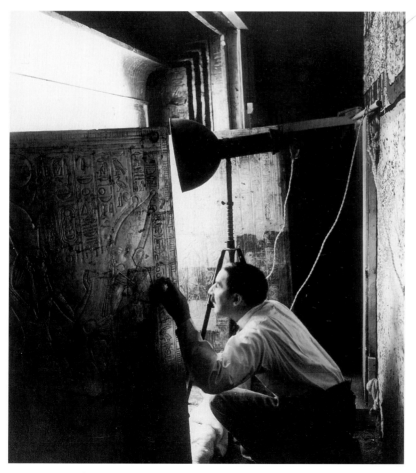

Howard Carter searched for six years before he found the tomb of the pharaoh Tutankhamen.

Adjoining this room was another, containing the mummy of Tutankhamen, in a series of wooden and stone coffins, one within another. There were also two other rooms, filled with still more treasures. This tomb had not been robbed like all the others, although it was found that robbers had once broken into it but had apparently taken only a few small items. Thus, this was one of the greatest archaeological finds in history. Among

▲ ARCHAEOLOGY CAN FILL IN GAPS IN HISTORY ▲

Egyptian history that has been preserved tells us that in 1570 B.C. (3,567 years back from the year 1997) most of Egypt was being ruled by people known as the Hyksos. *Hyksos* is an Egyptian word meaning "chieftains from foreign countries." In other words, Egypt was occupied and ruled by foreigners.

The part of Egypt that wasn't controlled by these foreigners was ruled by an Egyptian prince named Seqenenre. The Egyptians wanted their whole country back, and according to the bits of history we have, the Egyptians drove the Hyksos out of Egypt in 1570 B.C. and Seqenenre's son, named Ahmose, became the first king of what is known as the New Kingdom of Egypt.

But what became of Seqenenre? Did he lead the battle against the Hyksos? Was he killed? The bits of history left don't give any information.

However, in 1881, archaeologists discovered a number of mummies of Egyptian kings and nobles, with their names clearly marked on the coffins. And one of them was none other than Seqenenre.

In 1886, Seqenenre's mummy was unwrapped, and what was found was shocking. Seqenenre's body was covered with wounds! A sharp weapon, probably a spear, had been thrust into his head, below his left ear. There were three deep gashes, made by axes, in his forehead. His nose had been smashed by a blow from some kind of club.

It seems clear that Seqenenre *had* fought in a battle to drive the Hyksos from Egypt. He had probably commanded the Egyptian army. But he hadn't survived the fight. It looks as if one of the blows or stabs to his head knocked him down and then he was hacked to death while he was on the ground.

So, the discovery of a mummy provided answers to several questions. Archaeology had filled in a gap in history.

the more than 5,000 objects in the tomb were carved wooden chests, beds, chairs, clothing, game boards, four complete chariots, and other things providing priceless information about Egyptian artistry, workmanship and technology.

THE ROYAL TOMBS OF UR   In the late 1920s, the tombs of a number of ancient Sumerian kings and queens were discovered in Iraq by another English archaeologist, Leonard Woolley, who was excavating the 5,500-year-old city of Ur. Like the Egyptians, the Sumerians buried things for use in the afterlife in the tombs of their rulers. These tombs contained objects as exciting and precious as those found in Tutankhamen's tomb: the golden headdress of a queen, the gold helmet of a king, musical instruments ornamented with designs in gold and the semiprecious blue stone called lapis lazuli, a gold and lapis lazuli statue of a goat, a lapis lazuli panel inlaid with figures of soldiers and chariots in mother-of-pearl and shell.

But in this great graveyard of royalty that Woolley and his workers excavated from 1926 to 1934, they found evidence that some rulers of ancient Ur required more than just objects of metal and stone to accompany them in their afterlife. They apparently demanded that the *people* who had

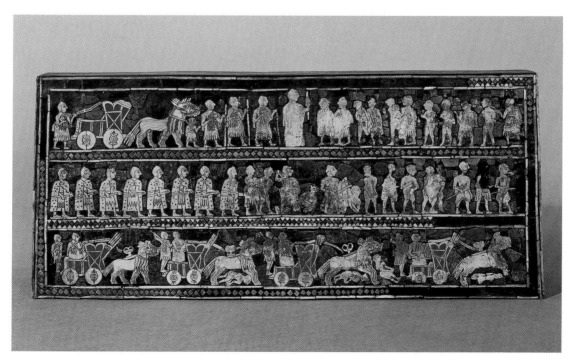

Leonard Wooley discovered this lapis lazuli panel, called the Royal Standard of Ur.

This is the headdress and jewelry of Pu Abi—one of the court women of Ur.

served them in life must serve them in death as well. During the excavations, Woolley's workers uncovered one tomb in which seventy-four human skeletons lay on the floor, along with skeletons of oxen and donkeys and the remains of chariots. Some of these skeletons were those of soldiers, rusting helmets still on their skulls and their bony hands clutching spears. Others were obviously court women, in elaborate gold headdresses. Several had been musicians; they were holding the remnants of musical instruments. It looked as if all these people had calmly entered the tomb, in which a dead king had been placed, lain down on the floor, and probably taken poison. The animals must have been killed by having their throats swiftly cut. When all were dead, the tomb had been sealed. All these people—soldiers, courtiers, musicians, chariot drivers—had deliberately sacrificed themselves to accompany their king into his afterlife, where they could continue to serve him. A number of similar tombs were found, with a total of 640 skeletons of people who had given up their lives for their rulers.

Nothing like this was ever found in any other Sumerian tomb. It was Woolley's opinion that the royal tombs of Ur were extremely ancient, and that as time passed, the custom of requiring people to accompany a ruler in death was done away with. However, even this gruesome custom served a purpose in helping provide information on the craftsmanship and technology of ancient Sumer.

THE TOMB OF CHINA'S FIRST EMPEROR

In 1974, two farmers in the Shensi province of central China were digging a well when they suddenly began uncovering the life-size, hard-clay statue of a man dressed in what was obviously ancient clothing. They quickly notified authorities, and within days, Chinese archaeologists were swarming over the area, making a major excavation. What they found was something sensational. Within an area the size of a small city, some 7,500 figures of ancient soldiers—spear bearers, archers, horsemen, officers, and even an imposing general—were unearthed from the soil, standing row upon row in military formation. The soldiers were armed with real weapons of bronze, and each man's face was distinctly different from all the others.

How these figures got there was no mystery to the archaeologists. Ancient Chinese legends tell that an army of terra-cotta soldiers was assembled in corridors dug 20 feet (6 meters) underground, to guard the tomb of the first emperor of China, who was buried about 2,200 years ago. The archaeologists realized that the two well-digging farmers had accidentally discovered the army of statues. The ancient legend was true!

The first emperor, known as Ch'in Shih-huang-ti, was a king of a small country who conquered a number of other small countries, unifying them to form the basis of what is now the nation of China. He was the emperor who caused the incredible Great Wall of China to be built. It is known that the emperor's tomb is within a 164-foot (49-meter)-high mound that rises about three quarters of a mile (1.2 kilometers) from the pits where the sol-

The restoration of the terracotta army of China's first emperor will keep archaeologists busy for years to come.

diers stand. The tomb of the Emperor Ch'in will someday be excavated, and it will probably be the most magnificent tomb ever uncovered by archaeology. Ancient legends say that 700,000 people worked on it for many years, that it contains untold riches, and that it boasts such marvels as rivers of quicksilver (mercury) flowing through parts of it. Inasmuch as the legend of the army of clay soldiers turned out to be true, archaeologists believe these legends are probably true as well.

THE TOMB OF A PHARAOH'S SONS

Among the many tombs in Egypt's Valley of Kings is one that has long been known as Tomb Number 5. It was investigated by an Englishman, James Burton, in 1820. He judged that it was simply a big area that had probably been looted by tomb robbers thousands of years before and now was filled with rubble and contained nothing valuable. In later years, archaeologists working nearby used Tomb Number 5 as a dumping place for debris their workers dug up.

Today, the Valley of Kings is a great tourist attraction, and in the late 1980s Egyptian authorities decided a parking lot was needed in the area. As Tomb Number 5 was of no importance, they determined the parking lot could go right on top of it, which, of course, would seal it up completely. However, Dr. Kent Weeks, an American Egyptologist, felt that the tomb should be carefully checked one last time before this happened. In 1988, he and his assistants began digging a long, narrow tunnel through the rubble.

Because of his regular job as a professor at a university in Cairo, Dr. Weeks could work at the dig for only a few weeks each summer. Finally, in May of 1995, as fragments of stone were removed from the end of the tun-

---

▲ A MESSAGE FROM ONE ARCHAEOLOGIST ▲ TO ANOTHER—ACROSS 168 YEARS!

When Dr. Kent Weeks began his attempt to find out whether there was something more to Tomb Number 5 than everyone believed, he examined the records of another archaeologist who had looked the tomb over 168 years earlier. This was the Englishman, James Burton, who had tried to tunnel into the tomb in 1820. Burton had uncovered three chambers, but found nothing of any importance and finally gave up. However, he had written a report about his efforts, and this document was one of the things that led Dr. Weeks to begin digging where he did.

Burton had written about finding a door that had the name of Pharaoh Ramses II carved on it. Following the directions in the report, Dr. Weeks located the door. Beyond it was a tunnel, choked with chunks of stone.

Holding his electric light up so that he could see the walls and ceiling, Dr. Weeks began to crawl through the tunnel. Suddenly, something on the ceiling caught his eye. There, written on the pale stone with the black soot of a candle, was the name of James Burton and the date 1820!

Burton must have believed that some other archaeologist would follow in his footsteps one day, so he had left a message—a message that said hello from one archaeologist to another, across 168 years!

Dr. Kent Weeks discovered the tomb of Pharaoh Ramses II in 1995. Note the statue of Osiris in the background.

nel, a door was revealed, a door that had obviously been sealed for thousands of years and that had been overlooked by earlier investigators of Tomb Number 5. Forcing it open, Dr. Weeks squirmed into a long corridor with rows of doors on each side. At the far end, in a niche carved into the rock wall, stood a statue of Osiris, the Egyptian god of the dead. The walls were covered with carved, painted figures; some crumbled away, but some had paint as fresh-looking as when it was first applied.

Dr. Weeks and his helpers had discovered that Tomb Number 5 is actually the largest and most elaborate of any of the tombs ever found in Egypt. It was built some 3,200 years ago by Pharaoh Ramses II as the burial place for his 50 sons. There was no treasure in the tomb, only broken fragments of jars and bits of beads, for the tomb was robbed about 3,100 years ago. No mummies or mummy cases were found, either. But Dr. Weeks believes there may be an entire lower level of the tomb, beneath what has been found already, and perhaps it will contain the mummies of Ramses's sons. Excavations will continue until this is determined.

Like lost cities, hidden graves and tombs of ancient kings and commoners will continue to be discovered, each one adding to the sum of information about our ancestors of long ago.

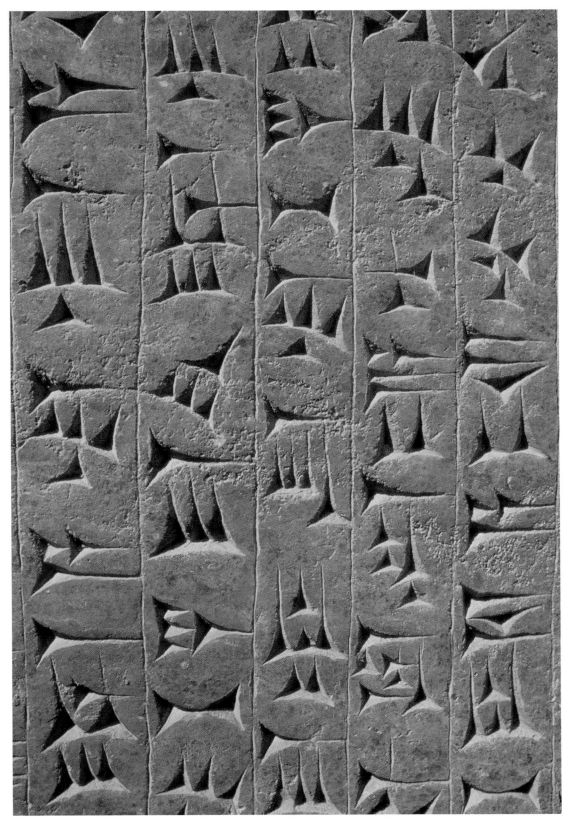

Cuneiform

▼▼▼▼▼▼▼▼▼▼▼▼▼▼▼▼▼▼▼▼▼▼▼▼▼▼

FOUR

WORDS FROM THE PAST

*T*he greatest portion of our knowledge of most ancient civilizations has come to us from the writings that were left behind by the people of those civilizations. Accounts of events in the lives of kings and queens have enabled historians to piece together the histories of ancient nations. Stories and legends have provided glimpses of the values and beliefs of ancient people. Even such seemingly unimportant things as merchants' records of items they bought and sold have been a source of considerable information about the everyday life of ordinary people, the kind of foods, clothes, and goods available to them, and how they bought and paid for what they wanted. But before archaeologists and historians could find out all these things, someone had to be able to *read* the ancient words. And at first, this had seemed impossible.

When scholars and travelers from Europe first began digging and delving among the ruins of the civilizations of ancient Egypt, ancient Assyria, and other long-gone nations of the Near East, they quickly realized that these nations had all had some form of writing. The Egyptians had used pictures and symbols to stand for sounds and words, and the ancient Greeks had named these hieroglyphics, or "holy carvings," because they could only be read by priests and temple scribes. The writing of Assyria and other ancient nations of the Near East was formed of wedge-shaped characters made by jabbing a chisel-like stick into pieces of soft clay, which were then baked hard in hot ovens. The Europeans named this kind of writing cuneiform, meaning "wedge-shaped." But even though the ancient civilizations had left many writings carved on palace and temple walls, inscribed on clay tablets, and painted on papyrus, a paperlike material made from plant stems, no one could read them. The languages of Egypt, Sumer, and Assyria were dead and gone, and so were those of most other ancient civilizations that were being uncovered around the world. Even to people who now lived where those civilizations had flourished, the languages were a mystery.

However, there were scholars whose main goal was to solve the mystery of ancient languages. The first ancient writing to be deciphered was that of the Egyptian hieroglyphics. It happened because of a French general, a stone slab, and a little boy who swore that he would do it.

SOLVING THE RIDDLE OF THE ROSETTA STONE
In 1798, the French General Napoleon Bonaparte invaded Egypt with an army of 35,000 soldiers. Napoleon was a well-educated, very intelligent person, and brought with him 175 scholars, historians, scientists, and artists, whose job was to collect, examine, write about, sketch, and make plaster casts of as many Egyptian antiquities as possible. In 1799, a group of Napoleon's soldiers working on a fort in a town called Rosetta dug up a large slab of black rock, 3 feet, 9 inches (114 centimeters) high and 2 feet, 4½ inches (72 centimeters) wide. One side of it was polished smooth and covered with carvings that were obviously writing. The officer in charge of the soldiers realized that Napoleon's group of scholars would want to see this and immediately sent it to the general's headquarters in the city of Cairo.

The stone quickly became known as the Rosetta stone. Napoleon's scholars saw that the writing carved on it was in three forms; the upper section was Egyptian hieroglyphics, the middle was an unknown type of cursive (connected) writing, and the bottom section was Greek, which many scholars could read. It was soon determined that the Greek writing was a record of the accomplishments of the Egyptian Pharaoh Ptolemy V, who ruled Egypt about 2,200 years ago. Greeks controlled Egypt at that time, and Ptolemy was a Greek, which was why the writing was in that language. Napoleon's scholars realized that the other two sections of the stone must repeat what the Greek section said, but in writing that Egyptians could understand.

Plaster casts were made of the Rosetta stone, and sent back to France. This was fortunate, because the stone itself was later captured by the forces of France's enemy, Britain. However, it was an 11-year-old French boy

The Rosetta stone is on display at the British Museum in London, England. The stone clearly shows three distinct bands of writing.

named Jean François Champollion who, upon hearing of the Rosetta stone, vowed to decipher the hieroglyphics on it. He grew up to be a genius with languages and began his attempt to solve the puzzle of hieroglyphics in 1808, at the age of 18.

Eventually, in 1822, Champollion solved the problem when he found two sets of hieroglyphics that seemed to match the names of King Ptolemy and his queen, Cleopatra, which appeared in the Greek text. What struck Champollion was that where the two *a*'s of the name Cleopatra would appear in the sixth and ninth positions, as written in Greek, there were two identical hieroglyphic symbols, a standing bird. These must be the Egyptian characters for an *a* sound, Champollion decided. He also saw that the hieroglyphic that was where the *p* should be in Cleopatra also appeared at the beginning of the other set of hieroglyphics, where the *p* for Ptolemy should be. And the symbol that appeared where the *o* in Cleopatra should be was exactly where *o* belonged in Ptolemy. Champollion now had three hieroglyphic characters for sure and was quickly able to figure out all the others simply by their positions in the names. He rushed to the library where his brother was working, yelled out "I have it! I have it!", and fainted dead away from excitement.

By matching many other hieroglyphic symbols to the Greek letters they represented, Champollion was able to translate the meanings of hundreds of Egyptian words. In 1824, he published a book describing his discoveries and showing how hieroglyphics could be read. In following years, scholars began to translate the hieroglyphics on thousands of sheets and scrolls of papyrus in museums all over the world, revealing information about Egyptian history, religion, customs, and ways of life. There was an explosion of knowledge about ancient Egypt. Sadly, Champollion did not live to see any of this. He died in 1832, at the age of only 42.

CUNEIFORM IS DECIPHERED
The work on deciphering cuneiform writing had actually begun six years before Champollion began his work on hieroglyphics. It was started in 1802 by a German schoolteacher named Georg Grotefend. Grotefend really didn't have much interest in archaeology, but one evening he made a boastful bet with some of his friends that he could learn to read cuneiform writing.

Grotefend had nothing to work with but a copy of a cuneiform inscription that had been taken from the ruins of a palace in the remains of an ancient Persian city. The first thing he had to figure out was the *direction* of cuneiform writing, that is, whether it was read from the right or left or from top down or bottom up. He did this by noticing that the points of the wedge shapes forming the characters of cuneiform always pointed either to the right or downward. He decided, correctly, that this meant they had been written from left to right, and from top to bottom. He was then able to determine that two groups of characters were the names of two Persian kings, Darius and Xerxes (known from ancient Greek writings). This showed him what sound each character in the name stood for. He later also worked out the name of a third king. Thus, Grotefend had deciphered twelve cuneiform characters and read the names of three kings written in cuneiform, so he had won his bet!

But Grotefend did not try to learn anything more, and archaeologists did not know of what he had done. So it was 45 more years before cuneiform was deciphered well enough to be read by scholars as Egyptian hieroglyphics were. The bulk of this work was done by an Englishman named Henry Rawlinson, who without knowing it actually repeated much of what Grotefend had already done. Like Grotefend, Rawlinson was able to find the names of Darius and Xerxes in cuneiform, but instead of stopping with that as Grotefend had, Rawlinson went on to use them as a stepping-stone to learn the sounds of many cuneiform characters. By 1847, he had become able to read Persian cuneiform fairly well, and by 1857, he had learned how to translate Persian into Assyrian and was thus able to read

---

▲ SOME OF THE OLDEST THINGS ▲ FOUND BY ARCHAEOLOGISTS

OLDEST DOOR The oldest known door, which dates back to about 6,000 years ago, came from the remains of a New Stone Age village that once stood beside a lake in Switzerland. It was made from a single piece of wood from a tree trunk, split into a thin rectangle, with several holes running down one side. It was probably attached to a doorpost by means of leather thongs running through the holes.

OLDEST SUIT OF ARMOR The oldest known European body armor, about 3,200 years old, came from a tomb in the ruins of Dendra, in Greece. The armor consists of a neckpiece, chest protector, "skirt," leg sheaths, and a wrist guard, all made of bronze. It also includes a helmet made of boars' teeth that were fastened onto a metal cap with bronze cheek protectors attached.

OLDEST PRINTED BOOK The earliest printed text known was found in 1907 among a library of Chinese writings discovered by Sir Aurel Stein. It was hand-printed in A.D. 868, more than 1,100 years ago, by means of wooden blocks on which Chinese characters were carved. The characters were coated with ink, then pressed onto the page.

Assyrian. With Rawlinson's work to guide them, scholars of the late 1800s began to put together the histories of Assyria and other nations of ancient Iraq and Iran.

One of the outstanding benefits that came from being able to read the writings of the ancient Near East was the discovery of one of the world's oldest and greatest pieces of literature, the Sumerian Epic of Gilgamesh. Written probably more than 4,000 years ago, it is the vast, exciting story of a king of Sumer named Gilgamesh who, with his close friend the superb warrior Enkidu, has many fantastic adventures. Together they slay the ferocious fire-breathing giant Humbaba and kill the great raging Bull of Heaven that is turned loose upon the world by the goddess Ishtar. The epic also contains a story of a titanic flood that is very similar to the story of the flood found in the Bible, but the Epic of Gilgamesh was written centuries earlier.

This impression, made by a cylindrical seal, shows the slaying of Humbaba—part of the Epic of Gilgamesh.

THE DISCOVERY OF THE HITTITE EMPIRE

In the year 1834, a Frenchman by the name of Charles Texier, who was much interested in archaeology, visited a little town named Boghazköy, in Turkey. Nearby, he saw the ruins of what had clearly once been a mighty city, with parts of the walls and great carved gates still visible. Some distance from these ruins, carved into the rock on the side of a cliff, was a weathered ancient sculpture showing figures who looked quite different from the Assyrians, Babylonians, or other ancient people who had lived near this region. And on the sculpture were some worn markings that looked as if they might be some kind of hieroglyphic writing. Texier was puzzled. He did not know of any ancient people who might have lived there. There were certainly no historical records of anyone building mighty cities and writing with hieroglyphics in this place. In 1836, he published a book describing what he had seen. Other archaeologists and historians who read it were as puzzled as he was.

Not long after, similar ruins and more of the unknown hieroglyphics were found in Syria, hundreds of miles from the place Texier had found in Turkey. It was clear to archaeologists and historians that there must have once been a great empire stretching from Turkey to Syria. But whose empire had it been?

In 1880, a young English scholar named Archibald Sayce provided an answer. He pointed out that in several places the Bible mentions people called Hittites who lived somewhere in the Near East thousands of years ago and were apparently as great a power as Egypt or Assyria were. Almost no one except a few Bible scholars even knew these people had ever existed, and absolutely nothing was known about them. But Sayce suggested that the great empire that had flourished in ancient Turkey and Syria was the empire of the Hittites.

At first, most historians scoffed at this. But then more clues came to light. Egyptian and Assyrian writings were found that referred to a "land of Hatti" in the northwest. A collection of letters on clay tablets was discovered, from a king of Hatti to his "brother" the pharaoh of Egypt. Finally, in 1906, German archaeologist Hugo Winckler, working in the ruins at Boghazköy, found some writings in the language of ancient Assyria, which he could read. They revealed that the ruined city, which had been called Hattusas, was the capital of the land of Hatti, which was indeed the Hittite Empire. Thus, almost by accident, a great ancient unknown civilization had been discovered, largely from writings that had provided the clues to its existence.

A reproduction of one of Charles Texier's drawings shows figures he found carved into the side of a cliff near Boghazköy.

Among the clay tablets found by Winckler were a number that were written in cuneiform characters, but in a completely unknown language—the language of the Hittites, which the Hittites usually wrote in hieroglyphs, of course. In cuneiform, the sounds of all the words could be read, but their meanings were a mystery. Much of the history and ways of life of the Hittites could be revealed if someone could learn to understand this cuneiform version of the Hittite language. A few scholars began to try.

The man who succeeded was a young Czech named Friedrich Hrozný. He began to study the writings and suddenly realized that the way the sentences were put together was very much like the grammar of Indo-European languages, a family of languages that includes many of the languages of Europe. Could Hittite be an Indo-European language? wondered Hrozný. Because Indo-European languages are descended from a single ancient language, most of them have a number of words that are very much alike, such as the word for mother—*mother* in English, *mutter* in German, *mater* in Latin, *meter* in Greek, and *madre* in Spanish. Hrozný began to look for Hittite words that seemed similar to words of Indo-European languages and quickly found many. In 1915, he was able to announce that Hittite was indeed an Indo-European language, and he had deciphered it!

Of course, the form of hieroglyphics with which the Hittites had done most of their writing still could not be read. But that problem, too, was solved before long. In 1947, German archaeologist Helmuth Bossert discovered a "Rosetta stone" for the hieroglyphics—a clay tablet with both Phoenician and Hittite hieroglyphics that said the same thing. Scholars could read Phoenician, so the Hittite hieroglyphics were easily translated.

Soon, the full story of the Hittite Empire was being revealed. At its height, this empire had indeed been as great and powerful as either Egypt or Assyria. It had conquered Babylon some 3,500 years ago and fought a titanic battle against Egypt about 3,300 years ago that resulted in peace between the two nations from then on. The Hittites were one of the first people to learn how to smelt iron, and they were successful in many ways. But around 3,100 years ago the Hittite Empire was invaded and destroyed by a vast horde of migrating tribes, and all knowledge of it became lost for some thirty centuries. Now much of the story of this great ancient empire has been restored to history, through the words its people left behind.

THE LANGUAGE OF THE MYCENAEANS

When Arthur Evans was digging into the ruins of Knossos, on Crete, he found a number of fire-hardened clay tablets inscribed with two different kinds of writing that became known as Linear A and Linear B. After the end of World War II, in 1945, a British architect named Michael Ventris became interested in trying to decipher Linear B using decoding methods that had been used to decipher German radio codes during the war. Most experts believed that Linear B had nothing to do with the Greek language, but after a time, Ventris began to think it might be a form of early Greek after all. When he began to apply his decoding methods to it as if it were Greek, understandable words suddenly began to appear. By 1952, Linear B had been fully decoded. It is the language of the Mycenaean civilization of ancient Greece. This discovery was proof that the Mycenaeans, who had many cities and kingdoms in Greece, had taken over the Minoan civilization on the island of Crete.

Somewhat unfortunately, the Linear B tablets from Knossos turned out to be mainly just ancient government records—lists of the names of officials, tabulations of imports and exports during a year, and so on. Linear B tablets found at other Mycenaean sites during the twentieth century were much the same. While this provides some information about Mycenaean ways, it does not offer any facts about Mycenaean history, which is still mostly unknown. The cause of the collapse of the Mycenaean civilization around 3,200 years ago is a mystery.

Linear A has not yet been deciphered. While its characters are much like those of Linear B, they represent a completely unknown language, probably the language of the Minoans. It seems as if some of the Linear A tablets may just be lists of things, as the Linear B tablets are, but other Linear A writings that have been found look as if they might be stories or even histories. Experts will continue to work on them in the future, and they may well be deciphered someday.

THE DEAD SEA SCROLLS

The Dead Sea is a lake of salt water that forms part of the border between the countries of Israel and Jordan, in the Near East. Steep cliffs rise above its eastern and western banks, and in 1947, an Arab shepherd boy exploring a cave in the cliffs made what has been called the greatest discovery of handwritten text in history. He found some rolled-up pages (scrolls) made of leather and papyrus covered with writing, which have become known as the Dead Sea Scrolls. During the next few years, archaeologists found more scrolls in other caves nearby. The scrolls consist of the oldest-known versions of books of the Old Testament of the Bible, and other religious writings, that were probably made about 2,000 years ago. Most are written in Hebrew and Aramaic, two ancient languages of the Near East, and some are written in Greek. Scholars think they may have been part of the library of a group of people known as Essenes, who were a Jewish religious sect of that time. The scrolls provide information on religious thinking in the time just before the birth of Christ.

THE LOST HISTORY OF THE MAYANS

The Mayans were a Native American people who created a magnificent civilization in the area

Caves in the cliffs above the Dead Sea yielded scrolls written in ancient languages of the Near East.

that is now Guatemala, Belize, and parts of Mexico, Honduras, and El Salvador. They were the only Native Americans who invented their own form of writing, using picture-symbols similar to hieroglyphics. When the Spanish conquistadores invaded the Mayan Empire in the early 1500s, they were astounded to find that these people had actual *books* similar to the books of Europe. Unfortunately, the Catholic priests who accompanied the conquistadores believed that these books contained only "superstition and lies of the devil," and so they had them ruthlessly burned and destroyed by the hundreds. Today, only four Mayan books remain in existence.

Had the Mayan books been spared, it would have been easy to learn the history of the Mayan Empire, for the Mayans could have shown the Spaniards how to read their written language. But with the destruction of most of the books, Mayan history was lost. When the Mayan Empire was rediscovered in the 1800s, archaeologists had to begin to try to learn to read Mayan hieroglyphics from the few books left. However, it was quickly learned that the Mayans had also left a great deal of historical information in hieroglyphics on nearly all of their carved stone statues and monuments. It took nearly a hundred years, but by 1991 Mayan hieroglyphics had been completely deciphered. Now the work of learning the history of this great ancient Native American civilization is in full swing.

ANCIENT WRITING, THE KEY TO THE PAST By recovering the writings of Egypt, Assyria, Sumer, Mycenae, the Mayans, and other great nations of the past, the world has been enriched. Learning the histories and customs of these people who were our ancestors is not only interesting and fascinating for many of us but can help humanity learn more about itself.

Of course, many of the languages of the past have not been recovered, and many of the mysteries that have tantalized generations may never be solved. The people who made the marvelous cave paintings 20,000 years ago and those who built Stonehenge 4,100 years ago did not leave any writings that can tell us why they did those things. The writing of the Etruscans, that of the people of the Minoan civilization, and that of Mohenjo-Daro are still all puzzles that most archaeologists fear may never be solved, so we may never know what the people who built those great civilizations knew and thought and believed.

But over the past hundred years and more, there have been some incredible scientific discoveries that have turned out to be of tremendous help to archaeologists. Perhaps an unforeseen discovery will be made that will somehow help us unlock the secrets of ancient languages. Perhaps archaeologists themselves will discover other "Rosetta stones" that will make it possible to decipher the language of the Minoans, or of Mohenjo-Daro, or of the Etruscans. We can be sure that new scientific and archaeological discoveries *will* be made in the future, and that we will continue to learn more and more about the people of the past—our ancestors who shaped the lives we live today.

GLOSSARY

afterlife   a life after death, as believed in by many religions

antiquities   objects that were made by people of ancient times

artifacts   objects that were made by people of any past time—prehistoric, ancient, or recent

Bronze Age   the period following the Stone Age, from about 5,500 to 3,000 years ago, when people in much of Europe, the Near East, and Asia made most of their tools and weapons out of bronze

context   the location where any remains or artifacts of people of the past are found

culture   the customs, beliefs, art, architecture, cooking, and general way of life of a large united group of people such as a tribe or nation

cuneiform   a type of writing in which words are formed by putting small wedge-shaped marks together in different ways

ecofacts   natural objects and substances, such as bones, seeds, and grain, that are often found in places where there were human communities

embalm   a method of filling a dead body with substances that help preserve it

excavation   in archaeology, the uncovering of buried remains of past civilizations and cultures by digging

features   remains of large, immovable constructions made by people of the past—buildings, roads, etc.

fossils   the remains or evidence of prehistoric animals or plants, generally preserved in a hardened form—bones, footprints, leafprints, petrified skin, etc.

grave goods   clothing, weapons, and various personal possessions put into a grave with a dead person at the time of burial

ground-penetrating radar   a form of radar that can send radio waves into the ground to locate buried ruins

hieroglyphics   a form of writing in which pictures represent words or sounds, or a combination of words and sounds

infrared photography   a type of photography that literally photographs the *heat* (infrared radiation) given off by things and can thus show images of objects that are warmer than their surroundings, even when they are buried underground

Iron Age   the time, beginning about 3,000 years ago, in which people have made most of their tools, weapons, machines, etc., from the metal iron

kiln   a special kind of oven for baking soft clay into pottery

Mesolithic   the so-called Middle Stone Age, from about 10,000 to 5,500 years ago, when bows and arrows and cutting tools became common throughout the world. Mesolithic means "middle stone."

mine detector   a device used by armies to detect buried mines (explosive charges in metal containers). It can also be used by archaeologists to find small metal objects buried close to the surface of the ground.

mummification   the natural or artificial preservation of a dead body by means of extreme dryness or extreme cold, sometimes aided by chemicals

Neolithic   the so-called New Stone Age, during which farming began and humans made their finest stone implements. In some places, it actually began at about the same time as the Middle Stone Age, and it ended about 5,000 years ago when people began to use metal. Neolithic means "new stone."

Paleolithic   the so-called Old Stone Age, from about 2 million to 10,000 years ago, during which humans made most of their tools and weapons from stone and lived by hunting. Paleolithic means "ancient stone."

Phoenicians   a Semitic people of the Near East who are given credit for the invention of the alphabet

prehistoric   the entire period of time before any history was written down

radiocarbon dating   a method of telling the age of once living materials by the amount of decay (loss) of radioactive carbon that has taken place in them

ranked society   a tribe, nation, etc., that is organized into nobles and commoners

Renaissance   the period in Europe from the 1400s to the 1600s, when there was a surge of interest in art, literature, architecture, and education, which ended the medieval period and ushered in modern times

site   a place or area that archaeologists believe may contain important remains or information

soapstone   a type of soft rock that has a slick, soapy feeling

Stone Age   the prehistoric period from about 2 million to 5,000 years ago, during which prehumans and humans made use of stone for tools and weapons

stratigraphic digging   digging that is done straight down through all the layers of earth containing artifacts and ecofacts

thermoluminescence dating   a method of telling the age of inorganic materials, such as rock and clay, by measuring the amount of light energy released when they are subjected to intense heat

TIME LINE OF MAJOR ARCHAEOLOGICAL EVENTS DISCUSSED IN THIS BOOK

YEAR	LOCATION	EVENT
1709	Italy	The buried ancient Roman city of Herculaneum is discovered.
1748	Italy	The buried ancient Roman city of Pompeii is discovered.
1780	United States	Thomas Jefferson makes the world's first modern-type archaeological excavation, of an ancient burial mound in Virginia.
1788	Scotland	James Hutton presents evidence that the earth is far older than has generally been believed.
1797	England	John Frere finds stone tools in a deep layer of earth and concludes there must have been primitive, stone-using humans living in an unknown prehistoric time.
1821	France	Jean François Champollion learns how to read Egyptian hieroglyphics from the Rosetta stone.
1836	Denmark	Christian Thomsen formulates the idea of three ages of human development—Stone, Bronze, and Iron.
1839	Honduras	John Lloyd Stephens and Frederick Catherwood find a lost city of the Mayan Empire.
1843	Iraq	Dr. Paul Emil Botta discovers the palace of the Assyrian King Sargon II. Unknown to him, it is only some 14 miles (22.5 kilometers) from the site of the great Assyrian city of Ninevah.
1847	Iraq	Austen Layard begins to excavate the site of Ninevah.
1853	Switzerland	The remains of a submerged prehistoric village are discovered in Lake Zurich.

Year	Location	Event
1857	Germany	The first remains—a skull and leg bones—of one of the prehistoric humans known as Neanderthals are discovered.
1868	France	Skeletons of modern-type humans of 30,000 years ago, now known as Cro-Magnons, are discovered.
1869	Iraq	Ancient clay tablets inscribed with cuneiform writing in an unknown language are unearthed. This is the first evidence of the lost civilization of Sumer.
1870	Turkey	Heinrich Schliemann locates the site of the fabled city of Troy, proving that it was not a mere legend.
1871	Zimbabwe (Africa)	Karl Mauch finds the abandoned city of Great Zimbabwe.
1876	Greece	Heinrich Schliemann uncovers treasure-filled Bronze Age tombs in the ruined city of Mycenae.
1877	Iraq	Ernest de Sarzec discovers the ancient Sumerian city of Lagash, and the world begins to learn about the people and culture of Sumer.
1879	Spain	Awesome paintings made on cave walls by prehistoric artists are discovered.
1900	Crete	Sir Arthur Evans uncovers the remains of an ancient civilization that he names Minoan.
1900	Mediterranean Sea	The first statue by a famous ancient Greek artist (Lysippus) ever to be found is taken from the remains of an ancient Greek ship sunk off the Island of Andikithera.
1908	France	The grave of a teenage Neanderthal boy is discovered.
1911	Peru	Hiram Bingham discovers the remains of the Incan site now known as Machu Picchu.
1915	Czech Republic	Friedrich Hrozný deciphers Hittite cuneiform writing.
1920	Egypt	For the first time, aerial photography is used to locate ancient buried cities in the Sinai Desert.
1921–22	Pakistan	The cities of Harappa and Mohenjo-Daro are uncovered.
1922	Egypt	Howard Carter discovers the tomb of Egyptian Pharaoh Tutankhamen.

Year	Location	Event
1926–34	Iraq	Leonard Woolley discovers the graves of Sumerian kings and queens in the city of Ur.
1932	Italy	The remains of two Roman ships in Lake Nemi are raised to the surface.
1947	Iraq	Helmut Bossert deciphers Hittite hieroglyphic writing, bringing the history of the Hittite Empire to light.
1947	Israel	The Dead Sea Scrolls are discovered.
1949	United States	Chemist Dr. Willard Libby invents radiocarbon dating, making it possible for archaeologists to accurately date the ages of once living objects.
1952	England	Michael Ventris deciphers Linear B, the writing of the Mycenaeans.
1961	Sweden	The Swedish warship *Vasa*, which sank in 1628, is raised to the surface.
1961	Turkey	James Mellaart excavates the 8,300-year-old city of Catal Hüyük, the oldest city yet known.
1974	China	The 2,200-year-old tomb of China's first emperor is unearthed, containing an "army" of 7,500 life-size statues of soldiers.
1984	Turkey	A 3,400-year-old ship is found in waters off the Turkish coast.
1991	Italy	The naturally mummified body of a 5,100-year-old Stone Age man, with preserved clothing and possessions, is found in the melting ice of an Alpine glacier.
1995	Egypt	Dr. Kent Weeks uncovers the tomb of Egyptian Pharaoh Ramses II's 50 sons.
1995	United States	Using mine detectors, a college professor and students find the exact site of a 200-year-old American battle.

FOR FURTHER READING

Anderson, Joan. *From Map to Museum: Uncovering Mysteries of the Past.* New York: Morrow Junior Books, 1988. The story of an archaeological dig off the coast of Georgia, the methods used to uncover the artifacts there, and what was learned.

Cooper, Ilene. *The Dead Sea Scrolls.* New York: Morrow Junior Books, 1997. This account takes the reader from the initial discovery of the first seven scrolls, to the re-creation of the scrolls accomplished with computers in 1991.

Foster, Leila Merrell. *The Sumerians.* New York: Franklin Watts, 1990. Recounts how archaeologists discovered ancient Sumer and describes the way of life of the Sumerians.

Giblin, James Cross. *The Riddle of the Rosetta Stone: Key to Ancient Egypt.* New York: Thomas Y. Crowell, 1990. Describes how the discovery and deciphering of the Rosetta stone made it possible to read ancient Egyptian hieroglyphics.

Hackwell, John W. *Diving to the Past: Recovering Ancient Wrecks.* New York: Charles Scribner's Sons, 1988. Covers the field of marine archaeology, describing how archaeologists locate, explore, excavate, and preserve ancient shipwrecks.

Lauber, Patricia. *Tales Mummies Tell.* New York: Thomas Y. Crowell, 1985. An explanation of how the study of the mummies of Egypt, Peru, and Denmark, both man-made and natural, can reveal information about ancient civilizations.

Lazo, Caroline. *The Terra Cotta Army of Emperor Qin.* New York: New Discovery Books, 1993. The discovery of the great "army" of life-size clay soldiers found buried near the tomb of China's first emperor.

Perl, Lila. *Mummies, Tombs, and Treasure: Secrets of Ancient Egypt.* New York: Clarion Books, 1987. An examination of the mummies and tombs of Egypt.

Perring, Stephania, and Dominic Perring. *Then and Now.* New York: Macmillan, 1991. By means of transparent overlays, readers are shown how famous ruined cities and monuments looked in their prime.

INDEX

ABOUT THE AUTHOR

Tom McGowen was born in Evanston, Illinois, reared in Chicago, and is a lifelong resident of the Chicago area. Married, he has four children and eleven grandchildren.

Mr. McGowen is the author of nearly fifty books for children and young adults, a body of work that includes both fiction (chiefly fantasy and science-fiction) and non-fiction. Two of his books have been named Outstanding Science Trade Books for Children; one has been selected as a Notable Children's Trade Book in the Field of Social Studies.

Mr. McGowen is a member of the Author's Guild. In 1990 he received the Children's Reading Round Table's annual award for "outstanding contributions to the field of children's literature."